LOIS HOLE'S Rose Favorites

LOIS HOLE'S Rose Favorites

BY **LOIS HOLE**

WITH **JILL FALLIS**

PHOTOGRAPHY BY

AKEMI MATSUBUCHI

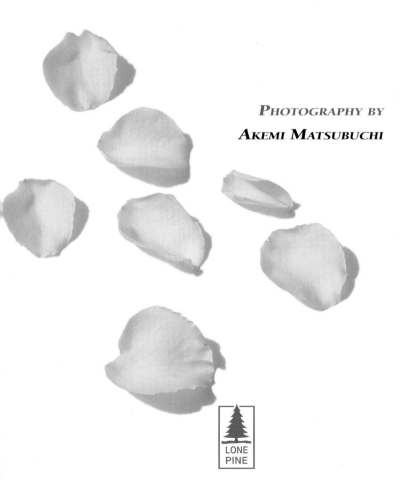

LONE PINE

The Publisher: **Lone Pine Publishing**

#206, 10426-81 Ave.	202A, 1110 Seymour St.	16149 Redmond Way, #180
Edmonton, AB	Vancouver, BC	Redmond, Washington
Canada T6E 1X5	Canada V6B 3N3	USA 98052

Canadian Cataloguing in Publication Data
Hole, Lois, 1933–
    Lois Hole's rose favorites
    Includes bibliographical references and index.
    ISBN 1-55105-079-X

    1. Roses—Canada. 2. Rose culture—Canada I. Fallis, Jill,
1960– II. Matsubuchi, Akemi, 1967– III. Title. IV. Title: Rose favorites.
    SB411.5.C3H64 1997   635.9'33372'0971   C96-910892-3

Senior Editor: Nancy Foulds
Project Editor: Lee Craig
Design and Layout: Bruce Timothy Keith
Production Management: David Dodge, Carol S. Dragich
Proofing: Lee Craig, Roland Lines
Cover Design: Carol S. Dragich
Printing: Quality Color Press, Edmonton, Alberta
Prepress: Screaming Colour, Edmonton, Alberta
Principal Photography: Akemi Matsubuchi
Additional Photography: Agriculture and Agri-Food Canada–L'Assomption, Quebec,
    p. 139 (top); Alberta Agriculture, Food and Rural Development, Crop Diversification Centre, Brooks, AB, p. 57 (top); Alberta Environment Centre/Hugh Philip,
    p. 58 (right); Rich Baer, pp. 112, 182 (top), 195 (top & bottom), 204, 206, 236,
    241 (bottom); Ted Brown, pp. 220, 223, 241 (top); David Austin Roses, p. 235;
    John Dean, p. 73 (top); Mark Dicey, p. 73 (middle); Valerie Hole, p. 135; L.L.
    Lozeau, p. 27 (bottom); Marianne Majerus/Garden Picture Library, pp. 97;
    compliments of Dr. Ian Ogilvie, 82 (bottom); Photos Horticultural Picture Library,
    pp. 88, 110, 115; compliments of Robin Rose, p. 70 (top).

Photographs on the following pages were taken in the garden of Donald Heimbecker, of Calgary, Alberta: 12, 19, 31 (bottom two),46, 98 (top), 127 (top), 156 (bottom), 187 (top), 207 (top), 214 (top).

The recipe for the frozen rose bowl (p. 84) was supplied by Vicki Wilson. The recipe for rose petal ice cream (p. 70) was supplied by Robin Rose, of Robin Rose Ice Cream & Chocolate, Venice, California. The recipe for 'Panache of Wild Greens with a Rose Petal Vinaigrette' (p. 166) was supplied by Chef Raymond Taylor, of the Hotel Macdonald, Edmonton, Alberta.

We have made every effort to correctly identify and credit the sources of all photographs, illustrations and information used in this book. Lone Pine Publishing appreciates any further information or corrections; acknowledgement will be given in subsequent editions.

The publisher gratefully acknowledges the support of Alberta Community Development and the Department of Canadian Heritage.

ACKNOWLEDGMENTS

*'He who would have beautiful roses in his garden
must have beautiful roses in his heart.'*
—SAMUEL REYNOLDS HOLE (1819–1904),
FIRST PRESIDENT OF THE ROYAL
NATIONAL ROSE SOCIETY, ENGLAND

The information within this book comes
from many kind people who generously
shared their wisdom. From Agriculture
Canada, we would like to thank Dr. Neville
Arnold and Dr. Ian Ogilvie (now retired),
of L'Assomption, Quebec, and Dr. Campbell
Davidson, of Morden, Manitoba. Special
thanks to Brad Jalbert, of Select Roses,
Langley, B.C., and to Don Heimbecker, of
Calgary, Alberta, whose impressive roses
appear in many of our photographs. Thanks
also to all the gardeners who allowed us to
photograph their gardens, and in particular
to Annabel Martindale, Joan Parker and
Kathy Feniak. Thank you to Vicki Wilson for
her stunning rose bowl, and to Jenni Lecuyer
and Amy Leach for their splendid rose candles. Thank you to Stewart Parker, who
believes that roses are more than just
flowers, and who provided an assortment
of rose jams, teas and rosewater, as well as
showing us his rose stamp collection.
Special thanks to Brian Minter, who
generously provided the beautiful flowers
that you see in the cover photograph.

CONTENTS

Introduction 9
The Rose Garden 11
    What Is a Rose? 11
    Finding a Path to Roses 14
    Choosing Which Roses to Grow 16
Planning the Rose Garden 19
Where to Plant 25
Buying Roses.. 29
    Three Ways to Buy Roses...................... 30
Planting Roses 33
    When to Plant 33
    Before You Plant 33
    How to Plant Roses 34
Filling Your Garden with Roses..................... 37
    Climbing Roses 37
    Rose Hedges 38
    Tree Roses... 40
    Groundcover Roses 41
Growing Roses in Patio Pots 43
Caring for Roses with a Minimum of Effort 47
    Watering 47
    Fertilizing 49
    Pruning 51
    Deadheading 54
    Pest Control 54
    What to Do in Fall, Winter & Spring 61
    Making the Most of Your Roses 65
    Bouquets of Roses................................. 65
    Drying Roses 68
    Potpourris 69
    Cooking with Roses 70
    Attar-of-Roses 72
    A Guide to the Varieties 75
    FAVOURITE HARDY ROSES 79
    FAVOURITE TENDER ROSES 161
    Appendix 243
    Select Glossary 250
    For More Information 250
    Bibliography 251
    Index 252

FAVOURITE ROSE VARIETIES

Hardy Roses

Adelaide Hoodless 85
Agnes 86
Alain Blanchard 87
Alba Maxima 88
Alba Semi-plena 89
Alchymist 90
Alexander Mackenzie 91
Autumn Damask 92
Blanc Double
  de Coubert 93
Botzaris 94
Cabbage Rose 95
Captain Samuel Holland 96
Celestial 97
Champlain 98
Charles Albanel 99
Charles de Mills 100
Cuthbert Grant 101
Dart's Dash 102
David Thompson 103
Double White Burnet ... 104
Euphrates 105
F.J. Grootendorst 106
Fimbriata 107
Frau Dagmar Hartopp . 108

Frontenac 109
Frühlingsanfang 110
Frühlingsgold 111
Frühlingsmorgen 112
George Vancouver 113
Hansa 114
Hebe's Lip 115
Henry Hudson 116
Henry Kelsey 117
J.P. Connell 118
Jens Monk 119
John Cabot 120
John Davis 121
John Franklin 122
Kakwa 123
Louis Jolliet 124
Mme. Hardy 125
Marie Bugnet 126
Martin Frobisher 127
Max Graf 128
Morden Amorette 129
Morden Blush 130
Morden Cardinette 131
Morden Centennial 132
Morden Fireglow 133

Morden Ruby 134
Nigel Hawthorne 135
Nozomi 136
Pavement Roses 137
Quadra 139
Red Frau
  Dagmar Hartopp 140
Red Rugosa 141
Red-leaf Rose 142
Reine des Violettes 143
Rosa Mundi 144
Scabrosa 145
Schneezwerg 146
Simon Fraser 147
Stanwell Perpetual 148
Superb Tuscan 149
Sweetbriar Rose 150
The Hunter 151
The Polar Star 152
Thérèse Bugnet 153
Topaz Jewel 154
White Rugosa 155
William Baffin 156
Wingthorn Rose 157
Winnipeg Parks 158

Tender Roses

Abraham Darby 167
Apricot Nectar 168
Aquarius 169
Charles Austin 170
Charles Rennie
  Mackintosh 171
Cupcake 172
Dainty Bess 173
Double Delight 174
Electron 175
Elina 176
Elizabeth Taylor 177
English Garden 178
Escapade 179
Europeana 180
Evelyn 181
Eyepaint 182
Fair Bianca 183
First Edition 184
First Prize 185
Fisherman's Friend 186
Folklore 187
Fragrant Cloud 188
Garden Party 189
Gene Boerner 190
Gertrude Jekyll 191

Glamis Castle 192
Gold Medal 193
Graham Thomas 194
Granada 195
Gruss an Aachen 196
Heritage 197
Iceberg 198
L.D. Braithwaite 199
Lilian Austin 200
Little Artist 201
Livin' Easy 202
Loving Touch 203
Magic Carrousel 204
Mary Rose 205
Minnie Pearl 206
Miss All-American
  Beauty 207
Mister Lincoln 208
Nearly Wild 209
Olympiad 210
Painted Moon 211
Paradise 212
Pascali 213
Paul Shirville 214
Peace 215
Peach Blossom 216

Pink Parfait 217
Pristine 218
Queen Elizabeth 219
Rainbow's End 220
Redouté 221
Regensberg 222
Rise 'n' Shine 223
Royal Highness 224
St. Patrick 225
St. Swithun 226
Sally Holmes 227
Secret 228
Sexy Rexy 229
Showbiz 230
Snow Bride 231
Sonia 232
Starina 233
Sunsprite 234
The Alexandra Rose 235
The Countryman 236
The Pilgrim 237
Tiffany 238
Touch of Class 239
Trumpeter 240
Winsome 241

INTRODUCTION

'Won't you come into the garden?
I would like my roses to see you.'
—RICHARD B. SHERIDAN
(1751–1816), ENGLISH DRAMATIST

At the start of every year, while the snow still blankets the ground, I look forward to the first sign of spring. At our greenhouse, it arrives about the middle of January, when our annual shipment of new roses comes in—all 10,000 of them. The roses are shipped in 'bare-root' form, which means, unsurprisingly, without soil. If you have never seen a rose in this form, you might be hard pressed to imagine beautiful flowers coming from these gnarled little stumps and twisted masses of roots, but trust that it will happen.

While the snow drifts outside, our team of five or six workers, all wearing thick gloves and long sleeves, gathers inside the long potting room and gets to work. Each of the 10,000 roses must be sorted and pruned by hand, soaked, trimmed and potted into fresh soil mix. In a matter of weeks it is done. By the time warm spring weather arrives, the roses have been growing inside our greenhouse for a couple of months, transformed into leafy bushes, some of which are already bearing flowers.

THE ROSE GARDEN

*'Oh, no man knows through what
wild centuries roves back the rose.'*
—WALTER DE LA MARE (1873–1956), ENGLISH POET

There is more interest in the rose than in any other single species of plant. Every year in Canada, more than 38 million roses are produced for sale as cutflowers. Approximately 700,000 rosebushes are grown for sale as plants, and still more are imported from Europe and the United States. In England, where the rose is the national flower, four out of five gardeners grow roses. There, and in other warmer parts of the world, garden roses are understandably taken for granted, because the English and other gardeners do not have to cope with long, cold winters, as we do in most parts of Canada and the northern U.S.

But roses can easily be grown here, and I look forward to the day when four out of five northern gardeners, as we call ourselves, will grow roses. I often hear from gardeners who exclaim that they won't grow roses because they are too much work, too fussy, too hard to grow. It's just not true! Perhaps this perception of 'no bed of roses' results from a lack of information. There are a lot of rose gardening books, but few are written specifically for areas where snow stays all winter.

The purpose of this book is to show you just how easy it is to grow roses. I will promise you a rose garden, one that provides beauty and bountiful bouquets, fragrance and flowers, with not much more effort than it takes to grow any other type of plant.

A rose is one of the most beautiful flowers both in the garden and in bouquets. It is also one of the oldest plant species, having been around longer than man has been on earth. Fossil remains indicate that a primitive form of the rose existed over 32 million years ago. Throughout history, all over the world, roses have been cherished more than any other

Once upon a time, in the days of yore, a goddess arose from the sea. This exquisite beauty was Venus, the goddess of love. Upon seeing her, Earth became jealous. Vowing to create something of equal loveliness, Earth combined the most rapturous fragrance with the most lovely form, thus bestowing upon mankind a great gift: the rose.

WHAT IS A ROSE?

Over 3000 years ago, the Greek poet Sappho pronounced the rose to be the 'Queen of Flowers.'

✳ *For centuries in England, the mention of a rose in the contract of a rental agreement meant a pledge of faith to the landlord.*

flower; heralded as an emblem of beauty, festivity and love; surrounded by myths and legends; and embellished with medicinal powers and magical attributes. For thousands of years, the rose has reigned supreme as a source of inspiration for poets, artists and lovers. No other flower has been so beloved and honoured.

History of Roses

Roses were first cultivated in China more than 5000 years ago. The first written record dates back to the Greek historian Herodotus. The Greeks have been credited with bringing roses to Europe. During the decadent days of the Roman Empire, fountains gushed with fragrant rosewater, beds and pillows were stuffed with rose petals, and banquet halls were lavishly decorated with the flowers. The emperor Nero is said to have spent the equivalent of $100,000 on cut roses for a night's entertainment.

Throughout Europe in the Middle Ages, roses were grown in monasteries for medicinal purposes. By the 1700s, more than one-third of all herbal remedies used roses—rose vinegar to relieve headaches, for example, and syrup-of-roses as a purgative. In the early 1800s, British trading ships returning from

It is easy to tell by looking at a rosebush whether or not it is grafted. The graft is where the desired rose variety was joined to a rootstock rose; it looks like a swollen lump near the bottom of the main stem.

China brought home roses along with their cargo of tea. Breeders used these 'tea-scented' or China roses to produce other roses, including hybrid teas.

How Roses Are Created

It takes, on average, 7 to 10 years to develop a new rose variety, and the odds of creating one that is better than those already available is said to be 300,000 to 1. Rose breeders often start out by cross-pollinating: brushing the pollen from one variety onto the stamens of another. It usually takes many crosses and many years before anything new and exciting results. Some of the world's largest rose nurseries—Jackson & Perkins, Weeks Roses and Conrad-Pyle—sow several hundred thousand rose seeds each year, in hopes of creating a wonderful new variety.

Once a promising new rose is produced, it's a matter of propagating enough plants to meet the demands of gardeners. The fastest way to do this is by *graft-ing*—joining one rose onto the roots of another rose. Another method of grafting roses that is becoming more and more common is *budding*—inserting a leaf-bud of one rosebush under the bark of a 'rootstock' variety. Either way, the rootstock rose may be slightly hardier, but usually the main reasons for joining one

One rosehip contains as many as 40 to 50 seeds. Only a small percentage of these seeds will germinate. Some rose seedlings bloom when only 4–5 inches (10–12.5 cm) high, but others take a year or two to produce flowers. If you want to try growing roses from seed, harvest when rosehips change colour. Chill seeds for two to three months in moist soil in the refrigerator, and then plant them into moist, warm soil. They should germinate and sprout about eight weeks after planting.

rose with another are better colour and improved growth habit.

Roses are sometimes also propagated by *cuttings*—pieces cut from a rosebush's stems are rooted and grown into new rosebushes. One cutting grows into one rosebush, but if that same cutting were budded, it could yield six to eight leaf-buds, which means six to eight rosebushes. Budding is also faster—cuttings take twice as long to grow.

Most roses sold have been propagated by grafting. Gardeners needn't be overly concerned with which method of grafting was used, for all grafted roses should be planted in the same manner (see *How to Plant Roses* on page 34).

FINDING A PATH TO ROSES

'Roses are red, violets are blue ...'
There are at present no truly blue roses, but breeders are attempting to create one by inserting a petunia's blue gene into the rose genes.

Years ago, when my husband Ted and I first started out on our farm, our primary focus was vegetables. Of course we also grew a few flowers and shrubs, and I particularly remember a big, old shrub rose beside our vegetable garden at the edge of the lawn. My boys and their friends used to love playing football, and they often crashed into the poor rosebush during their games. It pretty much ignored their intrusions, and undaunted, continued to produce its fragrant flowers summer after summer.

Although Ted and I started out growing and selling fresh vegetables, over the course of the years, our focus changed. We began producing annual bedding plants—flowers and vegetables—for sale, and gradually added more and more varieties, then perennials and finally, trees, shrubs and roses. Today our sons have joined the family business, and together we

A beautiful, fragrant rose garden is a real delight.

There are, at times, unexpected perks with a job; for one letter-carrier in St. Albert, Alberta, his 'bonus' is guaranteed each summer. As soon as he rounds the corner with his mailbag on a particular route, he is hit by an overwhelming, heady perfume that wafts down the street. Its source is the lavish garden at Stephen Raven's home. Stephen (above) grows over 250 varieties of roses. Neighbours often remark on the fragrance, which lingers in the early evening air throughout summer.

operate one of the largest greenhouses and garden centres in western Canada.

We are fortunate to have among our greenhouse staff many very knowledgeable people, including a young man whom I have known since he was a boy. Stephen Raven is an avid gardener, with hundreds of perennials and over 250 varieties of roses in his park-like garden. Roses are Stephen's passion, and he has contributed much to this book. Stephen is currently a regional director of the Canadian Rose Society.

Shane Neufeld is our nursery manager, in charge of trees, shrubs and roses. Based on Shane's knowledge, experience and instincts, the number of woody plants that we grow has increased immensely, and we have discovered some very intriguing varieties of roses. Shane, too, was an integral part of the creation of this book.

CHOOSING WHICH ROSES TO GROW

Today there are thousands and thousands of roses to choose from. The genus *Rosa* is one of the most extensive in the plant kingdom, although botanists do not agree about the total number of species (*species*, not varieties or cultivars)—claims range from 30 to over 5000.

Add to that tens of thousands of individual varieties, within the species, and the choice of roses is overwhelming. Every gardener who grows roses has favourites, which may or may not be included within my own favourite varieties listed in this book. This book does not include a comprehensive list of all rose varieties, but instead introduces those that I consider to be the best. I have grown and loved many of these varieties for years.

Where I live, the basic difference between rose varieties comes down to whether or not they are able to survive winters on their own. Those varieties that can are grouped as **hardy roses**; those that need a protective mulch covering so they can survive winter are grouped as **tender roses**. Refer to the listings on pages 85–158 and 167–241 for detailed variety descriptions.

The rose is the national flower of England, Honduras, Iran, Poland, Romania and the United States. It is also the official state flower of Georgia, Iowa, New York, North Dakota and the District of Columbia.

This one-of-a-kind rose was discovered on a hilltop near Montreal by a L'Assomption research station employee. The rose, which is so far nameless, will likely be used in the Canadian rose breeding program.

The Hope for Humanity rose was bred specifically to celebrate the 100th anniversary of the Red Cross.

❋ *I live in Alberta, Canada, where the official provincial floral emblem is the wild or prickly rose* (Rosa acicularis), *the largest and most widespread wild rose in this country, gracing woodlands from Quebec to British Columbia.*

Great Rosarians

For more than 26 years, George Pagowski has been in charge of the rose garden at the Royal Botanic Gardens, Hamilton, Ontario. There are over 170 varieties within the hugely successful garden, half of which are hardy roses. George played a key role in their introduction.

'And I will make thee beds of roses …'
—CHRISTOPHER MARLOWE (1564–93),
ENGLISH POET AND DRAMATIST

Although roses can be grown in their own area, I prefer them mixed in with other flowers. Place pots of roses on your balcony or patio, edge a flowerbed with a low, spreading variety, or grow a climbing rose beside your front doorway. With larger varieties, create a hedge of roses, mingle roses in shrub borders, or plant roses at the back of flowerbeds, with annuals and perennials growing in front.

Statues add elegance to the rose garden.

For a list of the best roses for hedges, see page 39. For a list of climbing roses, see page 38, for groundcovers see page 41, and for a list of the best roses for cutflowers, see page 67.

When I first started growing roses, I thought they were all pretty much the same—but they aren't. Roses bloom at different times, in various colours, on shrubs of many shapes and sizes. With so many varieties to choose from, there is surely a perfect rose for every garden. I talk to a lot of gardeners, and find that what most people want from roses is flowers all summer, fragrance and lots of colour. With that in mind, consider the following when planning your garden.

For Flowers All Summer …

Most gardeners want a continuous show of flowers from their gardens, and the best way to achieve that is to grow all sorts of different plants. Few roses bloom non-stop all summer; most take breaks—some varieties longer, some shorter—between peak flowering periods. If you want roses in bloom all summer, it's a good idea to grow more than one variety.

*'June brings tulips, lilies, roses
Fills the children's hands with posies.'*
—**traditional rhyme**

Some roses bloom only once each season, and I am surprised that this is a deterrent to quite a few gardeners. After all, roses are shrubs, just like a lilac or a hydrangea. No one expects these other shrubs to bloom all summer, so why should we expect it of roses? Once-blooming roses are among the most spectacular shrubs when they are in full flower; these roses put everything that they have into one glorious burst of bloom, rather than producing the same amount of flowers over a longer period.

For Fragrance ...

Roses are expected to be fragrant; few people pass by a rosebush in bloom without bending over to smell its flowers. Make the most of fragrant roses by planting them along a walkway, near an outdoor seating area or under a window that is often open, so you can enjoy the scent from both indoors and out. Choose a sheltered site where wind will not whisk away the perfume.

Fragrance differs from variety to variety; some roses smell sweet while others smell spicy. The scent can change as flowers age, and the same variety may seem more fragrant in one garden than another. Fragrance, like other features—the number of flowers or overall health of the bush—is affected by the amount of sunlight, water and fertilizer the rose receives, as well as the quality of the soil.

Rose scent is often compared to spices, licorice, honey, violets or other flowers, and fruit—apples, citrus or raspberries. As well, there are standard descriptions that may seem mystifying to anyone who has not smelled a lot of roses:

myrrh fragrance is spicy yet sweet with an almost medicinal punch
old rose fragrance is sweet with floral overtones, and is often called the 'true rose' scent
tea rose fragrance is fresh and sweet.

Roses and clematis make a lovely pair, and are often grown together in warmer areas, with the vine climbing through the branches of the rose. In cooler climates, such as where we live, it is best to choose a large variety of rose, like the Sweetbriar, which reaches a height of about 10 feet (3 m) at maturity. Delay planting the clematis until the rose is well established, because a young rosebush may be overwhelmed by the more vigorous vine. Late-flowering clematis, such as viticellas and texensis types, are good choices.

Although roses are famous for fragrance, not all roses emit that fabled perfume. Fragrance is a recessive trait, and in the breeding of many varieties, it has been exchanged for floral beauty, colour, long blooming season, disease resistance or hardiness. If a variety is outstanding in appearance or vigour, don't reject it just because it has little fragrance. With unscented roses, I often grow other fragrant flowers nearby: a carpet of sweet alyssum under a red rose, vanilla-perfumed heliotrope close to a pink rose or spicy-scented cottage pinks with a white rose. For a list of the most fragrant varieties, see page 249.

Flower fragrance changes with the weather. Scent is strongest on sunny days when the air is calm and moist, just after a summer rainshower and often following a light frost. Roses reputedly have the most heavenly scent just before sunrise— that's when flowers are picked for the perfume industry.

For Favourite Colours ...

Roses bloom in a wide array of colours, in shades from pastel to neon-bright. Within each colour category you'll find a range of hues: red roses, for example, vary from dark crimson to brilliant scarlet. Flower colour does, however, vary from garden to garden. It is affected by many factors, including variations in sunlight, temperature, soil and geographical region. See page 243 for a listing of roses by flower colour.

'Don't restrict your roses to the rose garden.'
—**American Horticultural Society**

F.J. Grootendorst contrasts beautifully in both texture and colour with the foliage of spruce.

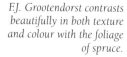 *Rosehips won't form unless flowers are pollinated. If weather is cool and rainy during the pollination period, few rosehips will form.*

More Than Just Flowers ...

Roses have more to offer than simply flowers. Certain roses are chosen primarily for their foliage. The Red-leaf Rose has stunning reddish-purple leaves that add unique colour to gardens. The foliage of the Sweetbriar Rose, on the other hand, doesn't look that different from most roses, but it has a lovely fresh-apple fragrance. The foliage of the variety Hebe's Lip has a similar scent. If you want a truly unique plant for your garden, choose the Wingthorn Rose. Its huge, hooked thorns are looped along the length of its branches, and gleam like rubies on a bright summer's day.

As a general rule, to create a pleasing show, grow roses in groups of two or three. Large shrub roses are an exception; just one rosebush provides a multitude of flowers.

Favourite Roses for Fall Colour

With the arrival of cool evenings in fall, the foliage of some varieties turns fiery shades of yellow, gold, orange and red, providing a showy display equal to that of maples or other shrubs grown for their colourful fall foliage. The following varieties are among the best for fall colour.

Blanc Double de Coubert
Charles Albanel
Dart's Dash
Fimbriata
Frau Dagmar Hartopp
Hansa
Jens Munk
Pavement Roses

Red Frau Dagmar Hartopp
Red Rugosa
Scabrosa
Schneezwerg
Thérèse Bugnet
White Rugosa

Scabrosa's foliage turns bright orange-yellow in fall.

Favourite Roses for Showy Rosehips

Rosehips vary from small to large, from deep red to bright orange, and from round to oval. They can remain on branches for several months, providing an incredibly beautiful display in fall. As well as providing fall colour, the formation of rosehips helps to prepare the rose for its dormant period in winter. The following varieties have the showiest display of rosehips.

Adelaide Hoodless
Alba Semi-plena
Blanc Double de Coubert
Celestial
Dart's Dash
Double White Burnet
Frau Dagmar Hartopp
Frühlingsanfang
Frühlingsmorgen
George Vancouver
Hansa
Jens Munk
Kakwa
Louis Jolliet
Morden Centennial
Red Frau Dagmar Hartopp
Red Rugosa

Red-leaf Rose
Scabrosa
Schneezwerg
Sweetbriar Rose
Thérèse Bugnet
White Rugosa

Don't deadhead species roses, such as the Red-leaf Rose (below). Doing so stops them from forming decorative rosehips, a great part of their appeal. The rosehips hang on branches well into winter, and make a stunning display against a snowy background as well as providing food for birds.

WHERE TO PLANT

> 'Where you plant a rose,
> my lad, a thistle cannot grow.'
> —FRANCES HODGSON BURNETT
> (1859–1924), AMERICAN WRITER

Roses like sun. Ideally, choose a site in the garden
that receives from 8 to 10 hours of direct sunlight
each day. Afternoon sun is preferable to morning
sun, because it's warmer—warmth encourages better
growth. In a site that is partially shaded for the best
part of the day, most rosebushes will be spindly with
fewer flowers; in full shade, they will slowly die.

The best type of soil for roses is loam: a balanced
mixture of sand, silt, clay and organic matter. Loam
is well-drained soil, meaning that water neither
puddles on top nor drains through too quickly. Work
lots of organic matter, such as peat moss, well-rotted
manure or compost, into your soil before planting to
improve both water and nutrient retention.

✳ In Flin Flon, Manitoba, roses grow—and flourish—1197 feet (365 m) below ground!
A mined-out chamber in a zinc and copper mine owned by the Hudson Bay Mining and
Smelting Company has been transformed into an underground garden, with computer-
controlled light, humidity, water and fertilizer.

Surround yourself with roses to enjoy their fragrance and beauty up-close.

With white roses, such as Botzaris, avoid planting in sites that are subjected to hot afternoon sun. In my experience, white flowers last longer out of the heat.

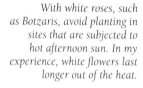 *Each spring, millions of tiny white blossoms cover the world's largest rose at Tombstone, Arizona. The Lady Banks rose (Rosa banksiae) stands only 9 feet (2.7 m) tall but its trunk is 40 inches (1 m) thick, and its branches cover an area of 5380 square feet (484 m²). Underneath this arbour, there is seating for up to 150 people! This famous rose is more than a century old; it was grown from a cutting imported from Scotland in 1884.*

Air movement is important for optimum health. Gentle breezes keep the foliage dry; most diseases that affect roses are more prevalent when foliage is moist for extended periods of time. Fungal diseases, such as powdery mildew and blackspot, are worse in sites with poor air movement.

The Winnipeg Parks rose beside my son Bill's house produces abundant flowers with only morning sun.

Red Rugosa is a very shade tolerant species.

Shade-tolerant Roses

Most roses need full sun, but some varieties do well even with shade for half the day. Remember, though, that 'tolerate' means 'will put up with but doesn't like.' Shade-tolerant varieties bloom in partial shade, but with fewer flowers than if grown in full sun.

Alain Blanchard	Gruss an Aachen
Alba Maxima	Mme. Hardy
Alba Semi-plena	Nozomi
Botzaris	Red Frau Dagmar
Cabbage Rose	Hartopp
Celestial	Rosa Mundi
Charles de Mills	Scabrosa
Double White Burnet	Schneezwerg
Frau Dagmar Hartopp	The Hunter
Frühlingsanfang	White Rugosa
Frühlingsmorgen	Wingthorn Rose

Great Rosarians

Claire Laberge is head horticulturist at the Montreal Botanic Gardens, one of Canada's finest public gardens. The huge rose garden attracts thousands of visitors every year.

'They that have roses never need bread.'
—DOROTHY PARKER (1893–1967), AMERICAN WRITER

These days, you can buy rosebushes just about anywhere. I have even seen roses for sale at a gas station!
While the good people at the gas station may know a
lot about cars, I'd be doubtful that they could offer
as astute advice about roses. It is important to consider quality as well as the source when shopping for
roses. A plant that has been poorly cared for before
you buy it is unlikely to fare well once it is planted
into your garden. The best sources are people who
specialize in plants. They know what the plants need
to keep them healthy.

*One rosebush usually costs less than a bouquet of long-
stemmed roses, and provides far more than a dozen flowers.*

*Rosebushes are most often sold either as container-grown
shrubs (left), or in bags (right). Always choose the healthiest,
lushest rosebushes, and avoid any with long, pale shoots.*

1. Boxed or Bagged Roses

• Roses are available from different sources in bags or boxes. Your selection may be limited, since often only the most common, mass-produced varieties are available.

• This is the least expensive way to buy roses.

✳ *Sometimes your newly purchased rosebush may have waxed stems. The wax prevents moisture loss during shipping. Don't worry about removing it; the wax will disintegrate on its own after the rose is growing in your garden.*

2. Bare-root Roses

• Bare-root roses are what you usually get from a mail-order supplier. They come in plastic bags filled with moist sawdust or peat moss.

• It is very important that the roots be kept consistently moist and cool before planting. Bare-root roses should be planted as soon as possible in spring.

• Bare-root roses must not be subjected to freezing temperatures during shipping. Rosebushes that have been frozen often produce shoots after transplanting, but die rather quickly. Unfortunately, it is difficult to tell whether a rose has been frozen before it is planted.

• This is the next most inexpensive route.

3. Container-grown Roses

The healthiest plants produce the healthiest blooms.

• These rosebushes are fully leafed-out, well-rooted and often already in bud or bloom.

Nursery manager Shane Neufeld checks the lush growth on young container-grown roses.

- Container-grown roses can be planted at anytime throughout the growing season, from early spring until a few weeks before the ground freezes in fall.

- You can feel confident that you are getting top-grade rosebushes. (Top-grade roses are larger, and won't fit into bags or boxes.)

- This type of rose is more expensive because it has a fully established root system, and has been actively growing in the pot.

Great Rosarians

Who says that you can't grow hybrid tea roses on the Prairies? Donald Heimbecker, of Calgary, Alberta, grows close to 400 of the most outstanding roses anywhere. He has been experimenting with different methods for 50 years. Many of the hybrid tea roses in his garden are over 14 years old!

'Time brings roses.'
—PORTUGUESE PROVERB

WHEN TO PLANT

I generally recommend spring as the best time to plant roses. It will give the rosebushes the entire growing season to establish themselves. As a result, they will better withstand stressful conditions. Plant roses in your garden as soon as the danger of hard frosts has passed.

Boxed, bagged and bare-root roses must be planted in spring. Container-grown roses, on the other hand, can be planted at anytime during the growing season, up until two to three weeks before the ground freezes in fall.

BEFORE YOU PLANT

'The Rose doth deserve the chiefest and most principall place among all floures whatsoever ...'
—GREAT HERBAL OF 1560

Before you plant boxed, bagged or bare-root roses, they should be given a little pampering to help them get the best start in the garden. Be sure to keep the roots moist at all times. The day before planting, soak them in a bucket of water for about 12 hours. Container-grown roses are ready to be planted as soon as you bring them home.

Shane Neufeld prepares to plant a container-grown rose.

HOW TO PLANT ROSES

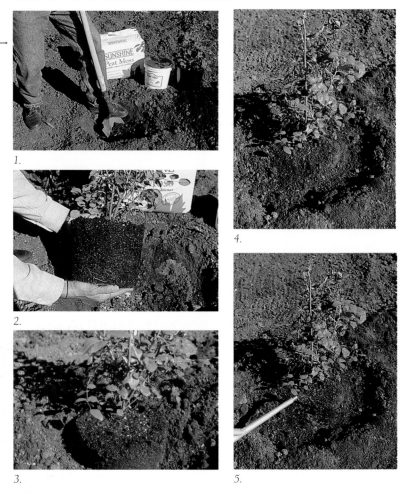

1.

2.

3.

4.

5.

Before you plant any rose, take note of its mature size, so that you will allow sufficient space. If possible, plant in the morning or evening to lessen transplant shock.

1. *Dig a planting hole that is wider and deeper than the container in which the rose is growing. Mix lots of organic matter—peat moss, compost or well-rotted manure— with the soil. Stir in a handful or two of bonemeal, to aid root development.*

2. *Remove the rosebush from its pot. Gently untangle the rootball to enable the roots to spread into the soil as the rosebush grows.*

3. *Set the rose into the planting hole.*

4. *Refill the planting hole with your mix of soil and organic matter, and firmly pack the soil around the stem, leaving a small depression around the base of the rosebush.*

5. *Water until soil is completely soaked. Newly planted rosebushes should be watered regularly and thoroughly once a week during the first growing season. Fertilize once a month with 20-20-20 until the first of August.*

Special Care for Tender or Grafted Roses

Tender varieties of roses are usually grafted: that is, the rosebush has been attached to the roots of a different, usually more vigorous rose. Most hardy roses are grown on their own roots, but if you do have a grafted hardy variety, plant it in the same manner as you would a tender rose.

Prepare to plant as on page 34, except to dig a deeper planting hole. Tender roses must be planted deeper than hardy roses. The colder the climate, the deeper the graft should be planted. In Alberta, where I live, and in Saskatchewan, Manitoba and northern Ontario, roses should be planted so that the graft is 4 inches (10 cm) below the soil line. In southern Ontario, on the other hand, and in parts of B.C., the graft needs to be only 2 inches (5 cm) below soil level. Planting with the graft properly buried is one of the most important steps in ensuring that tender roses survive winter.

In cold climates always bury tender rose grafts to the proper depth.

Special Care for Bare-root and Boxed Roses

Prepare to plant as on page 34, digging the planting hole large enough to enable the roots to spread fully. If your rose is tender or grafted, ensure that the hole is deep enough so that the graft will be buried to the recommended depth.

Make a mound of soil at the bottom of the planting hole and sit the rose on top, with its roots spread out over the mound, like a little octopus. Finish planting as on page 34. Fertilize with 10-52-10 once a week for the first three weeks after planting to help the roots become established.

Mulching them halfway up the stems with peat moss for one to two weeks improves water uptake.

✳ Thorns & Roses
It is said that the rose had no thorns until after Adam and Eve left the Garden of Eden. The Greeks claimed that the red rose came from the blood of the goddess Aphrodite whose foot got stuck on a thorn while trying to help Adonis. The Turks, on the other hand, held that the red rose is stained from the blood of Muhammad.

When planting bare-root roses, spread roots evenly for the best growth.

'When pleasure's blooming season glows,
the graces love to twine the rose.'
—THOMAS MOORE
(1779–1852), IRISH POET

Climbing roses are beautiful, with an abundance of flowers cascading overhead. These roses can quite easily be attached to a trellis, arbour, archway, pergola or fence. The easiest climbing roses to grow—in my area at least—are the hardy ones. I don't bother growing tender climbing roses, simply because it's far too much work to take them down from trellises each fall to ensure that they have adequate winter protection. Since there is such a wonderful selection of climbing roses that are both beautiful and hardy, I am very content to stick with these varieties.

CLIMBING ROSES

Growing

- Plant climbing roses in the same manner as other rosebushes. (Refer to page 34.)

- Roses need support because they don't have self-clinging or twining tendrils like many climbing vines.

- For the first two or three years after planting, don't prune climbing roses, except to remove deadwood or unwanted branches. The main objective during the first few years is to let the rose establish mature canes.

- Climbing roses that bloom only once each season, such as The Polar Star and Frühlingsmorgen, should be pruned after flowering. Repeat-blooming climbers, such as William Baffin and John Cabot, should be pruned in early spring while they are dormant.

- Prune climbing roses in the same fashion as other roses; refer to *How to Prune* on page 52.

Loosely tie the canes to a trellis. Use a soft material, such as foam-covered wire, string or strips of cloth. Never use bare wire because it can damage the rose.

William Baffin (left) and John Cabot (right) are two beautiful hardy Explorer roses at the home of Don and Anne Fleming, of Edmonton, Alberta.

Hardy climbing roses do not require winter protection. Leave them on their trellis or support, but be sure to water thoroughly in late fall.

Tips

• Climbing roses can look rather sparse near soil level. To brighten up that space, I love to plant colourful annual flowers around the base of my climbing roses.

• I often snip flowers from my climbing roses for short bouquets.

Favourite Climbing Roses

Alchymist	Louis Jolliet
Captain Samuel Holland	Max Graf
Frühlingsgold	Nozomi
Frühlingsmorgen	Quadra
Henry Kelsey	The Polar Star
John Cabot	William Baffin
John Davis	

ROSE HEDGES

'Wishing for roses, I walk through the garden ...'
—ANNA AKHMATOVA (1888–1966), RUSSIAN POET

I can't think of a nicer way to divide a property, line a driveway, create a windbreak or provide summer privacy, than with a hedge of roses. Shorter varieties, like Double White Burnet and any of the Pavement Roses, are good choices for smaller hedges. Large shrubs, such as Scabrosa and either White or Red Rugosa, make great barriers for privacy.

Growing

• If you are planting an entire hedge at once, the best way to do it is to dig a trench, which is easier than digging individual planting holes. It also results in roots becoming established more quickly and growing more vigorously. Make the trench about 18 inches (45 cm) wide and 15 inches (38 cm) deep. Otherwise, prepare the soil and plant the same as you would any rose. Refer to *How to Plant Roses* on page 34.

• Rose hedges are generally allowed to retain their natural shape. Space roses their full width apart, from centre to centre. With Hansa, for example, which spreads 4–5 feet (1.2–1.5 m) wide, allow 4–5 feet (1.2–1.5 m) between rosebushes.

Champlain makes a splendid low hedge, growing about 3 feet (90 cm) tall. This variety blooms non-stop until fall frosts, with abundant clusters of dark red flowers.

Favourite Hedge Roses

Adelaide Hoodless
Blanc Double de Coubert
Champlain
Double White Burnet
F.J. Grootendorst
Fimbriata
Hansa
John Franklin
Marie Bugnet

Morden Fireglow
Pavement Roses
Red Rugosa
Red-leaf Rose
Scabrosa
The Hunter
White Rugosa
Winnipeg Parks

TREE ROSES

Tree roses look terrific combined with colourful annual flowers.

Annabel Martindale over-winters her tree rose (right) every year in her garage. If you want to try this method, you need a garage with a consistently cold temperature (23°–32° F/-5°–0° C). The idea is to keep the rose in a dormant state; don't worry if its leaves fall off. Water your tree rose heavily in fall before storing it, and move it outdoors in spring.

Tree roses do not occur naturally—they are the art-work of a grafter or a pruner. With many tree roses, a rosebush is grafted atop a single, 2- to 5-foot (60–150 cm) tall stem. Less often, a larger shrub has been carefully pruned, so that all the lower branches are removed. Either way, the result is what looks like a small, pretty, flowering tree.

In recent years, hardy tree roses have become more widely available. My daughter-in-law Valerie has a Hansa tree rose, and I have seen lovely tree roses of Thérèse Bugnet and the Pavement Roses. Hardy tree roses grown in the garden are treated like other hardy rosebushes; they do not need winter protec-tion—unless they are grown in patio pots.

Most tree roses, unfortunately, are tender. I grow mine in patio pots, which look lovely and make winter protection much easier. Arrange the pots on your balcony, patio or deck. Alternatively, place them in the garden between other plants. A single tree rose makes a stunning centrepiece in a large flowerbed, and a pair of them on either side of a garden gate draws people into the garden.

Growing

- Tree roses are often sold staked, in pots. Leave the stake in place, as the stem is not strong enough on its own.

- Water often and heavily; roses growing in patio pots dry out very quickly! Patio pots should be checked daily.

- Be sure to fertilize regularly. I fertilize my potted tree roses once a week because the soil volume in pots is rather small and unable to hold enough nutrients for good plant growth.

- In fall, just before the ground freezes, dig a trench in your garden large enough to contain the entire tree rose. Ensure that the soil in the pot is evenly moist. Use a large sheet of burlap to keep the tree rose and its pot clean. Lay the burlap in the trench, set the tree rose horizontally into the trench on top of the burlap, wrap the burlap overtop, and bury it. Uncover in spring.

❋ *Tree roses are sometimes called rose standards.*

Many roses make wonderful groundcovers. Max Graf is one of the best, spreading as much as 10 feet (3 m) wide and only 2 feet (60 cm) tall. Its canes set root and sprout wherever they touch the ground, rapidly covering bare soil. Charles Albanel blooms all summer, and then turns bright orange in fall. Grow roses as groundcover wherever you want to cover a large area with flowers.

GROUND-COVER ROSES

'A rose is a rose is a rose is a rose.'
—GERTRUDE STEIN (1874–1946), AMERICAN WRITER

Growing

- Plant groundcover roses as you would any other rose. See *How to Plant Roses* on page 34.

- Groundcover roses won't suppress weeds like some of the very thick perennial groundcovers. To help reduce weed problems, lay a mulch of shredded bark under your roses.

Favourite Groundcover Roses

Charles Albanel
Dart's Dash
Double White Burnet
Euphrates
Frau Dagmar Hartopp
Max Graf
Nozomi
Pavement Roses
Red Frau Dagmar Hartopp

Max Graf

'And lovely is the Rose …'
—WILLIAM WORDSWORTH (1770–1850), ENGLISH POET

I love roses in all types of containers: patio pots,
window boxes and even hanging baskets. Many
roses grow well in patio pots, but only a few dwarf
or miniature varieties are suited to hanging baskets
and windowboxes. Experiment by combining other
plants with your pot roses: cascading lobelia, sweet
alyssum, trailing ivy or mealy cup sage, with its blue-
purple, upright flowerspikes. Use any decorative
container that you like, but keep in mind, roses are
not winter-hardy in patio pots.

GROWING

- The larger the container, the better, because you'll
  have to water less often, and the rose has more
  room to stretch out its roots. A five-gallon (23 l)
  pot is the minimum size for most roses. From the
  rose's perspective at least, bigger is always better
  when it comes to pot size. Remember, however,
  that larger pots are heavy and harder to move in
  fall, when you need to relocate them to provide
  winter protection.

- Use a good quality potting soil rather than garden
  soil to fill your pots. Garden soil is heavy and has a
  tendency to become rock-hard in containers, making it difficult for air, water and roots to penetrate.

- Roses in containers dry out surprisingly quickly.
  Check them every day without fail. Water often
  and heavily.

- Don't forget to fertilize regularly, too. I fertilize my
  pot roses once a week, with 20-20-20 added to my
  watering can. Potted roses need to be fertilized
  more often, because the soil volume in pots is
  rather small and unable to hold enough nutrients
  for good plant growth.

Supercascade Coral is an excellent trailing miniature rose.

• At the end of the season, you have three choices:

1. transplant the rose into your garden (about a month before the ground freezes in fall)
2. bring miniature roses indoors
3. provide winter protection.

Winter Protection for Pot Roses

You can protect your potted rose over winter by burying it in the garden, as you would a tree rose (see page 41). I recommend either wrapping the pot in burlap, or using a double-pot (grow the rose in a plain plastic pot set inside a more decorative pot for display on your patio).

Alternatively, wait until late fall when the rose becomes dormant, and then store it, pot and all, in a cold-room or heated garage. To keep the rose dormant throughout winter, it is important that the temperature remains constant—between 23°–32° F

Remember that roses in patio pots are not winter-hardy.

(-5°–0° C). Don't worry if the rose's leaves all fall off, and don't water the rose during its dormant period. Be sure, however, to soak the pot thoroughly just before you store it in fall.

Bringing Miniature Roses Indoors

Roses need a lot of light, so unless you have a very bright, sunny room or a solarium, you are unlikely to be successful growing roses inside your home. Miniature roses are the best candidates. Before I take my miniature roses indoors, I spray them with insecticidal soap to kill any aphids or spider mites.

Caring for Roses with a Minimum of Effort

'Stop and smell the roses ...'
—COMMON ADAGE

47

When people ask me what the secrets are to growing roses, I tell them to water once a week, fertilize once a month, prune once a year and deadhead once in a while. It's really just about that simple. Of course, some rose gardeners like to pamper their roses but it isn't necessary. Tender roses do also need extra winter protection (see page 62), but hardy varieties do not. Otherwise, the only demands roses make on your time is that you stop by often to admire them, to inhale the fragrance of their flowers, and to snip blooms for bouquets. Enjoy them every day.

WATERING

'... once a week ...'

Water roses regularly; they need more moisture than most plants. If you provide one gallon (4.5 l) of water per foot of height, once a week, you can't go too far wrong. More water less often is better than less water more often. Throughout spring and summer, water once a week.

Water less from early fall on, until a few weeks before freeze-up. Allow the soil to become slightly drier in order to slow down the roses' growth in preparation for winter.

Easy Ways to Reduce Your Water Bill
• Whenever possible, water early in the morning. Moisture loss through evaporation is far less in the morning than in mid-afternoon heat.

Roses need more water:
• *immediately after being transplanted*
• *throughout their first growing season*
• *when planted in south-facing beds*
• *while blooming*
• *in fall, just before freeze-up. Fall watering is an important step in ensuring that plants have the best chance for winter survival. Any plant that enters winter with its roots in dry soil is likely to suffer.*

Some roses are susceptible to powdery mildew, such as Garden Party (above). It is important to avoid wetting the foliage because wet foliage encourages disease.

My favourite watering tool is a water-wand—a terrific tool for providing a gentle flow of water just where I want it, on the soil. This inexpensive tool attaches to any hose. Most water wands come with a shut-off valve, which eliminates the need to run back and forth to the tap.

- Use lots of organic matter, like compost, peat moss and well-rotted manure, to improve the soil's ability to retain water. Add organic matter to the soil before planting, and supplement each spring and fall. Organic matter acts like a sponge: peat moss, for example, holds up to 20 times its weight in water.

- Build a rim of soil around rosebushes to create a saucer-like depression that holds water where it is needed.

- Trap water in rainbarrels for use in the garden.

Roses need rich soil for the best growth. Most garden soils contain all of the nutrients essential for plant growth, but often in insufficient amounts to suit the plants' needs. Regularly adding lots of organic matter, like compost or peat moss, helps tremendously. Usually though, I find the healthiest plants are the ones that are also fertilized on a regular basis.

There are several fertilizers designed specifically for roses. A common rose fertilizer is 28-14-14. The numbers indicate the major plant nutrients by weight; this fertilizer contains 28 percent nitrogen, 14 percent phosphate and 14 percent potash. These elements help plants in different ways: nitrogen promotes lush, leafy plant growth; phosphate promotes rooting and flowering; and potash helps with flower quality and disease resistance.

Fertilize roses once a month, in May, June and July. Don't fertilize after the end of July, which allows the rosebushes to slow down growth in preparation for winter.

There are two basic types of fertilizers: granular fertilizers, which you add directly to soil, and water-soluble fertilizers, which you mix with water, either in a watering can or with a fertilizer dispenser attached to the hose. Granular fertilizers release their nutrients over several weeks, and allow plants to grow vigorously but more slowly. Water-soluble

A quick way to apply granular fertilizer is with a broadcast spreader (left). A fertilizer applicator on your hose makes applying water-soluble fertilizers far easier (below).

Regular fertilizing helps to keep this Champlain rosebush healthy and blooming profusely.

fertilizers, on the other hand, release their nutrients quickly, and contribute to more rapid growth than the granular fertilizers. Either type is fine. Some gardeners prefer an annual application of fertilizer; others like fertilizing as they water. I like to use a combination of both.

Avid rose gardeners often develop their own individual fertilizer blends, and I hear of all sorts of interesting formulations, including everything from Epsom salts to recipes for compost tea. If it works for you, great! Many commercial fertilizers, however, are specifically formulated to meet the needs of roses, in both granular and water-soluble forms. I like to keep things simple, so I usually use 20-20-20 all-purpose fertilizer on all the flowers in my garden, including roses, with good results.

One other very important nutrient for roses is iron. Without iron, rose leaves can become very 'veiny.' If you have this problem, solve it by using a fertilizer that contains iron.

Bare-root and boxed roses have few roots, unlike container-grown roses, and can use a little boost to help them get going. Fertilize these roses with 10-52-10 plant starter fertilizer, immediately after transplanting and once a week for the next three weeks afterward.

Roses must be pruned at least once a year, so they will stay healthy and have many flowers. Tender roses generally need more pruning, and hardy roses need less pruning, other than the removal of any dead branch tips after winter. There is some debate about when is the best time to prune—in fall or in early spring—but in my opinion, it's simply a matter of which is most convenient. My son Bill prunes the roses beside his deck in fall, because their branches are likely to get broken as snow is piled overtop when the deck is shovelled during winter. The roses in his other flowerbed are left until spring to prune.

When to Prune

• Prune once-blooming roses shortly after they finish flowering. These roses bloom on old wood, which means that next year's flowerbuds form during summer. Don't prune in fall or early spring, because the result will be few flowers.

• Prune continuous and repeat-blooming roses either in fall or in early spring.

• Prune off damaged, diseased or broken branches throughout the year, as damage occurs.

Always prune to an outward-facing vigorous bud.

Two Good Reasons to Prune in Fall

- After pruning your tender roses in fall, you are left with a shorter bush to mulch (see *What to Do in Fall, Winter & Spring* on page 61) and no thorny branches to scratch your skin as you apply the protective mulch.

- There are no tall branches left that can sway in the wind and pull the protective mound of mulch apart. There will also be fewer leaves left on plants, which lessens the carryover of disease and insects.

Two Good Reasons to Prune in Spring

- If you prune your roses in fall, you may need to prune them lightly again in spring, just to remove any winterkilled branch tips. If you wait until spring to do your pruning, you won't have this extra step.

- During a mild winter, tender roses may not die back as much as they do during a harsher winter. By waiting until spring to prune, you may end up with taller rosebushes.

✹ *To prevent spreading disease, be sure to sterilize pruning shears with a mild bleach solution after using them on a diseased rosebush.*

How to Prune

Before pruning any rose, the first step is to find the tiny leaf-bud immediately above where a set of five or more leaves is attached to a cane. The rosebush will send out new growth from whichever direction that bud faces. Always make your pruning cut a short distance above an outward-facing bud, to avoid ending up with a lot of crossing-over, inward-facing branches, a situation that can promote disease. If there are already crowded or crossing branches on your rosebush, they should be entirely removed during pruning. Always use sharp shears and cut at a 45-degree angle rather than straight across the stem.

Dead branches (left) are common in the spring and should be removed (right).

Remember, each cut that you make affects your rosebush, whether you're gathering flowers, deadheading, or doing your annual pruning.

Winnipeg Parks is one of the most popular hardy shrub roses.

Hardy Roses

- Hardy roses need little pruning. Just remove the dead branches or branch tips in early spring.

- Once your rosebush is three to four years old, it's a good idea to remove one-quarter to one-third of the oldest, thickest canes. Prune them off at ground level to stimulate the growth of new canes, which will produce more flowers.

- Prune *once-blooming* roses after blooming. Prune *repeat-blooming* roses in fall after their leaves drop, or in early spring once their new leaves start to unfurl, but before they have fully opened. Follow the same rules for once- and repeat-blooming climbing roses.

- Pruning at the right time of year results in more flowers.

Whenever you are deadheading or cutting flowers for bouquets, be sure to cut the stem down to a leaf with at least five leaflets (the little leaves that make up a compound leaf).

Tender Roses

- If you are pruning in fall, cut rosebushes back to about 1 foot (30 cm) tall. Trim off any dead branch tips in spring.

- If you are pruning in spring, wait until the leaves begin to unfurl. Remove just the dead branches and branch tips.

DEADHEADING

'... once in a while ...'

Deadheading simply means removing dead flowers. This not only keeps gardens looking neat and attractive, it also prevents the roses from producing seed (which is contained within the rosehips) and thus stopping blooming. To keep roses blooming, remove finished flowers quickly. Snip off both spent single flowers and entire clusters.

Remember, though, to stop deadheading about four to six weeks before the average date of the first killing frost in fall. Where I live, a frost usually wipes out the garden sometime in October, so I know to stop deadheading towards the end of August. Allowing rosehips to form signals your rosebushes to prepare for winter.

PEST CONTROL

If you get into the habit of inspecting your roses closely and regularly, you will likely notice most pest problems before they become severe. I don't mind squashing bugs, and often just remove affected leaves to prevent insects or a disease from spreading onto other plants. A strong spray of water sends spider mites flying, and insecticidal soap works wonders on soft-bodied insects like aphids.

If you are constantly having a problem with a particular disease, consider replacing the rose with a disease-resistant variety. In my experience, however, many problems can be avoided by simply keeping the garden clean and the roses in the healthiest state possible. Powdery mildew is most likely to strike in areas with poor air circulation, where plants are too crowded and when soil has been allowed to dry out. Spacing plants further apart and improving watering practices may eliminate the problem.

Ironically, air pollution actually helps to prevent blackspot. Low concentrations of sulphur dioxide suppress this disease (gardeners often use a sulphur spray to control blackspot).

Insects often prefer plants that are weak or stressed. Enlist nature's help: be aware of and encourage 'good bugs,' such as ladybugs and lacewings, which feed on 'bad bugs' that damage plants. If you do run into a severe pest problem, take a sample leaf or other affected plant part into a garden centre whose staff can identify the problem and recommend the best treatment. Leaf spots or discolouration, for example, may result from a disease, but they can also be caused by a nutrient deficiency in the soil, or by frost, cold or severe lack of water.

Common Diseases

What are the black spots on the leaves of my rosebush?

This is one of the worst rose diseases: *blackspot*. This fungus causes leaves to get those dark spots, then turn yellow and fall off. Left unchecked, blackspot defoliates rosebushes from the lower leaves up, and it can sometimes kill roses. Blackspot is most prevalent on warm, humid days, at temperatures between 68°–75° F (20°–24° C).

The spores are spread by splashing water, and develop rapidly when they land on wet leaves, so when you are watering try to avoid wetting the foliage. Always water the soil, not the leaves! Pick up and dispose of fallen leaves, because they may harbour the fungus. Many rose varieties are resistant to blackspot.

What is that white powdery stuff on my rose leaves?

It is *powdery mildew*, a fungus that grows on the surface of foliage, coats the plant with white felt-like spores, causes leaves to curl up, and makes flowerbuds die without opening. Ugly as it is, powdery mildew does not kill most rosebushes, and many varieties are resistant.

The disease spreads fastest among drought-stressed plants when evenings are cool and the air is humid and still. The fungal spores germinate rapidly on leaves that have a coating of moisture, so do what you can to help keep the foliage dry. Space rosebushes far enough apart to allow good air circulation and don't let them dry out between waterings. I've found that keeping my roses as vigorous as possible with proper fertilization and lots of water keeps powdery mildew away.

The leaves of my rosebush are covered with reddish-orange spots. Why?

This is another fungal disease, called *rust*, which covers entire plants with tiny spores that resemble curry powder. Affected leaves wilt and fall off. Rust can defoliate and seriously weaken or even kill rosebushes. Luckily,

Most yellow roses are prone to blackspot, because they are descended from the wild Iranian rose, Rosa foetida. This species never developed any resistance to blackspot since the disease did not exist in its native habitat. Don't let this stop you from growing yellow roses, but do take particular care to water properly and keep the area around your rosebushes clean.

there are many resistant varieties, and when a rose is resistant to rust, it is almost completely immune to it (unlike blackspot, for which 'resistance' often simply means 'tolerance').

This disease occurs most frequently at temperatures between 64°–70° F (18°–21° C), accompanied by 4 to 12 hours of rain, fog or dew. Remove and destroy infected leaves. Rust is rarely seen east of the Rockies, but can be a serious problem on the West Coast. If you live there, it's a good idea to choose rust-resistance varieties. I've rarely found rust on my roses because our climate is quite dry and the humidity is often quite low during the growing season.

What is that lumpy, gnarled growth at the base of my rosebush?

A great lump near a rose's crown (the thickened junction of stem and root), graft or roots is usually *crown gall*. This disease is caused by bacteria and can be spread by infected tools, through soil or from plant to plant. When the bacteria invade the rose, they cause surrounding tissue to grow out of control, resulting in that big, lumpy growth. Crown gall causes plants to lose vigour, produce abnormal flowers and leaves, and eventually die. There is no cure. Remove and destroy the entire rosebush, including the roots and surrounding soil, to stop the disease from spreading.

My rose has weird circles and lines on its leaves. Why?

If those strange leaf patterns include bright yellow ringspots, lines and netting, the cause is *rose mosaic virus*, a complex of several viruses that attack roses. Rose mosaic virus weakens rosebushes, makes them abnormally sensitive to winter damage, and shortens their lifespans. There is no cure, and no varieties are known to be immune to it. However, affected rosebushes won't pass on the disease to others nearby, and they won't contaminate the soil. Still, you are best to get rid of them. Rose mosaic virus is most commonly transmitted from grafting onto virus-infected rootstock. Avoid it by buying your rosebushes from reputable sources.

Powdery mildew is one of the most common rose diseases. Avoid it by keeping rosebushes well-watered during dry spells, by not watering in the evening and by providing good air circulation. Many rose varieties are mildew resistant.

Rose mosaic virus spreads when roses are grafted onto infected rootstock, or cuttings are propagated from infected 'mother' plants.

Insect Pests

How do I get rid of aphids?

Aphids are small, soft-bodied insects (usually green) that suck plant juices from flowerbuds and new leaves. You do not have to eliminate every single aphid, but merely control their numbers. Insecticidal soaps work well and are safe to use. Ladybugs feed on aphids. Some garden centres sell lures to attract ladybugs to your garden, and also sell boxes full of live ladybugs!

What are the rounded swellings on the canes?

This is *rose gall*, caused by certain wasp species. The wasps secrete chemicals that cause the swelling, and each gall has a characteristic shape that identifies the species of wasp. As eggs hatch and larvae grow, the galls swell more. Prune off and destroy infected stems to eliminate the larvae before they emerge. Insecticides are not effective.

My rosebush's leaves are falling off. They are dry, stippled, and curled up; some have little spiderwebs on them. Why?

This sounds like *spider mites*, minute pests that suck juices from the undersides of leaves. These insects are most abundant in hot, dry weather. If there are just a few spider mites, I send them flying from my plant with a strong spray from the garden hose. If the problem is more severe, I use insecticidal soap, taking care to spray the undersides of leaves where the spider mites hide.

Rose gall is more common on species roses than on hybrid varieties.

Why are there holes drilled through my rosebuds?

Those perfect little holes are caused by the *rose weevil* (rose curculio), a very small insect about $1/4$ of an inch (5 mm) in length. With their long snouts, rose weevils bore into flowerbuds to feed and lay eggs. Remove and destroy affected flowerbuds.

The flowers on my rosebush are turning brown and only partially opening. Why?

Most likely, the culprit is *thrips*. These insects are hard to spot outdoors but easier to see indoors on your bouquets; you'll notice tiny, slender, dark brown or black insects emerging from inside the cutflowers, or crawling on your tabletop. Thrips damage, distort or destroy opening flowerbuds. If you suspect thrips, try this: cut off a couple of flowers, give them a hard rap overtop of a piece of white paper, and see if any thrips fall out. You can then spray your rosebushes with an insecticide, but often I just cut off and destroy the affected flowers.

My rose leaves have big circles cut out of them. Why?

Leafcutter bees cut perfect circles out of leaves, to create broad chambers for their larvae. They really don't cause much harm to the rosebush, but they do drive rose-exhibitors crazy! Leafcutter bees are not a serious problem—I just put up with them.

Aphids can be controlled using insecticidal soaps. Do not use detergent, because detergent can kill your plants.

Rose weevils create tiny holes in flowerbuds. They belong to a group of insects called Rhynchites, which have distinctive long snouts, similar to the horn of a rhinoceros. Remove and destroy any flowerbuds affected by this pest.

The American Rose Society voted spider mites 'most destructive' of all garden pests. These tiny insects can completely defoliate a rosebush in less than two weeks.

What are those slimy bugs eating holes in my rose leaves?

If they are dark green, about ½ an inch (1 cm) long and look a bit like slimy tadpoles, they are *pear slugs*—the larvae of sawflies. Pear slugs usually appear in early spring. They eat holes in leaves from the undersides, causing a skeletonized effect. The damage can be quite speedy, so react quickly. Pear slugs are among the easiest bugs in the world to kill: either brush them off and squish them, or spray with insecticidal soap.

Gardeners usually fight to keep bugs away from plants, but ironically, we were once involved in a life–and–death battle to find plants for insect fodder. At the Provincial Museum of Alberta in Edmonton (near my home), there is a permanent exhibit called the Bug Room, which just happens to be my grandson's favourite area. Michael is particularly fascinated by the walking–stick insects, and a few years ago, those insects were in peril of death by starvation. Walking–sticks and many of the other insects at the Bug Room are plant–eaters, but they only feed on certain types of plants. The museum has a greenhouse where plants are raised as a food source for the insects, but one cold night in February the boiler failed, and all the plants froze to death. Luckily, we were able to supply the museum with some rosebushes, enough to keep the insects in the pink until their own plant stock was restored.

WHAT TO DO IN FALL, WINTER & SPRING

'Gather ye rosebuds while ye may ...'
—ROBERT HERRICK (1591–1674), ENGLISH POET

WHAT TO DO IN FALL

- Remove any foliage that is infected with blackspot or powdery mildew. Be sure to pick up fallen leaves from the surrounding soil.

- Water heavily a few weeks before freeze-up— in my area, freeze-up occurs about late October. 'Watering-in,' as this is called, is important because it prevents roots from being damaged in cold, dry soil.

Many varieties of roses are valued for their colourful fall foliage.

❄ *Clean up the area around your rosebushes every fall. Pick up and dispose of any fallen leaves that may provide safe harbour for overwintering insect pests and disease spores. Fall clean-up is one of the most important steps in disease prevention.*

Additional Care
Required for Tender Roses

- Wait for frost to kill the foliage, and then prune rosebushes to one foot (30 cm) tall.

- Cover with a mound of peat moss to a minimum depth of 10 inches (25 cm). To prevent peat moss from being blown away, sprinkle a bit of soil overtop. Spray the surface of the mound with water, which will eventually freeze to form a crust. Keep the underlying peat moss and soil dry, to prevent the build-up of ice around the graft.

WHAT TO DO IN WINTER

- Whenever possible during winter, cover roses with fresh snow to prevent repeated thawing and freezing. Do not use hard snow or snow that contains salt or de-icer. Try to add more snow whenever shovelling walks; often only the branches exposed above the snowline die.

- Remember that all roses, even the hardiest varieties, benefit from having a good snowcover throughout winter.

WHAT TO DO IN SPRING

- Water rosebushes in dry, sheltered beds underneath house overhangs.

- As soon as the garden is dry enough to walk on, clear away any debris left from fall. Once leaf-buds break open and you can see what survived the winter, cut off the dead parts of branches.

Additional Care
Required for Tender Roses

- Watch the native trees. As soon as their leaf-buds start to swell, the area is pretty much safe from hard frosts until fall, and protective mulch coverings can be removed. Lift mulch off with your hands, rather than pulling it off with a rake, to avoid damaging tender new growth.

- Mulches must be removed sooner from garden 'hot spots' where snow melts early, such as flowerbeds against the south wall of your house. Check underneath those mulches fairly regularly. As soon as you see any signs of growth, remove the

Sweetbriar Rose

Use your hands (above) rather than a gardening tool to remove mulches so that you don't damage new growth.

mulch. If mulches are not removed at this point, the roses will start to produce growth that is weak and spindly.

- If there is a risk of frost within two or three days of removing the mulch, protect the newly exposed growth by covering your roses with an old sheet or blanket. Don't panic if you miss covering before an unexpected frost; freezing temperatures will damage only the newly exposed growth, not the entire shrub. Your rosebush will survive, but may be set back a bit and take longer to bloom.

- Prune tender roses in spring just after uncovering them. (See *Pruning* on page 51.)

Great Rosarians
The enormously popular Parkland rose series was developed on the Canadian prairies, at Agriculture Canada's Morden, Manitoba research station, by Campbell Davidson (left), Lynn Collicutt and Henry Marshall.

MAKING THE MOST
OF YOUR ROSES

'I'd rather have roses on my table
than diamonds on my neck.'
—EMMA GOLDMAN (1869–1940),
RUSSIAN-BORN AMERICAN ANARCHIST

BOUQUETS OF ROSES

Garden roses are lovely in bouquets, and are quite distinctive from long-stemmed florist roses. Whether in a vase all on their own or arranged with other flowers, I find bouquets of garden roses irresistible. Just because a certain variety is not recommended as a cutflower, don't let that stop you from trying those flowers in bouquets. I doubt that there is a rose in my garden from which I haven't snipped a flower or two, at one time or another.

How to Cut Roses

• I love those long-stemmed florist roses, but if you cut that much stem off the rosebush in your garden, be prepared to have very few flowers for the rest of summer. Taking a lot of stem from the rosebush seriously delays flowering. It's better to settle for shorter bouquets and more of them.

• Consider just snipping off a single flower to float in a rosebowl.

• After you bring the flowers inside, recut the stems at an angle to expose as much of the stem surface to water as possible. A fresh cut makes cutflowers last longer. Florists often cut the stems of roses underwater, to improve the water-uptake.

Tips

• Cut roses for bouquets either early or late in the day—they'll last longer than the ones picked in midday heat.

> 'The red rose whispers of passion
> And the white rose breathes of love;
> O, the red rose is a falcon,
> And the white rose is a dove.'
> —John Boyle O'Reilly (1844–90),
> Irish-born American poet

A dozen long-stemmed red roses are a sign of affection.

- Roses are often at their most fragrant in the morning.

- For the longest-lasting bouquets, pick single roses before they open, and double or semi-double roses just as they begin to open. 'Fully blown' flowers drop petals quickly after picking.

- Flowers picked at the 'tight bud' stage, when flowerbuds are still tightly closed, may not open any further after cutting. I think rosebuds are lovely in bouquets, and they often last as long as the open flowers.

- Generally, expect rose bouquets to last about a week. Varieties noted as 'long-lasting cutflowers' last 10 or so days, and a few exceptional roses last as long as two weeks!

- It's rather easy to tell whether or not a rose is a good candidate for cutting. Thick, almost waxy petals are characteristics of a good cutflower (this is described within the horticultural industry as a flower having 'good substance'). Few hardy shrub roses make good cutflowers, because they tend to have delicate petals.

- It is not necessary to remove thorns from cut-flowers, but if you want to, remove the thorns by simply pushing them sideways with your thumb. If you have a lot of roses to 'clean,' try an inexpensive florist's stripping tool. Certain roses, like many of the English varieties, have lots of small prickles that are not worth the bother of trying to remove. With those roses, I just wear gloves when picking the flowers.

- Remember to strip off any foliage below water level, because leaves decay quickly underwater.

Centuries ago, the language of love was flowers. Bashful suitors used to send messages through carefully constructed bouquets, in which each flower conveyed an individual sentiment. Here's what flower colours mean with roses:

red—true love, passion, desire
white—charm, innocence, purity
pink—simplicity, happy love
yellow—friendship, perfect achievement

When snipping flowers for bouquets, cut the stems just above the first set of five leaves, where new shoots will grow from. Make your cut at a 45-degree angle rather than straight across, which helps to prevent disease.

- Adding a floral preservative to the vase substantially increases the life of the cutflowers. Preservatives contain anti-bacterial compounds and 548 sugars, which can double vase-life.

The Best Roses for Cutflowers

Aquarius
Elina
Elizabeth Taylor
Glamis Castle
Gold Medal
Morden Fireglow
Mister Lincoln

Olympiad
Pascali
Peace
Sonia
Tiffany
Touch of Class

A rosebowl is a great way to show off your roses.

Great Rosarians

Miniature roses are as easy to grow as any other type of rose. Kathy Feniak, of St. Albert, Alberta, has 120 beautiful miniature rosebushes in her garden.

DRYING ROSES

'God gave us our memories so that we might have roses in December.'
—James Matthew Barrie (1860–1937), Scottish novelist

Roses are lovely in dried arrangements. The easiest way to dry these flowers is by air-drying: simply hang them upside-down, individually or in small bunches, to dry for about a week. The best time to pick flowers for drying is mid-morning, after the dew has dried from their petals.

Tips

• For best results, choose flowers that are open but not 'fully blown.' For variation in arrangements, dry a few rosebuds too.

• Unfortunately, the flower colours of roses often don't hold well when air-dried. Red roses tend to become quite dark, almost black. White roses usually turn beige, but still look attractive combined with dried flowers of other colours.

Air-dried roses glued to a wire frame create a stunning topiary.

Susan Bradley dries roses using silica gel and her microwave, a method that results in the flowers retaining perfect form.

Potpourri is a lovely mixture of dried, sweet-smelling flower petals. You can easily make your own by gathering fresh petals and flowers. Pick roses in the early morning after dew has dried from the petals. The fresher the flower, the more essential oil remains when it has dried. Gently pull off the petals from cutflowers, and place them on wire screen trays in a well-ventilated room to dry. Don't begin mixing potpourri until every petal is dry or you'll encourage mildew. Combine rose petals with anything you like: rosemary, lavender, dried and powdered orange skin, cloves and borage flowers.

※ *The rose has long been renowned as an aphrodisiac. Romans used to scatter rose petals on the bridal bed. Today this custom has evolved into throwing paper rose petals—or confetti—at weddings.*

POTPOURRIS

*'The rose looks fair,
    but fairer it we deem
for that sweet odour
    which doth in it live.'*
—WILLIAM SHAKESPEARE
(1564–1616),
ENGLISH PLAYWRIGHT AND POET

※ *For variety, add rosehips or whole rosebuds to potpourris.*

'Potpourri' is a French word meaning 'rotten pot'; pronounce it 'poe-poor-ee.' Ancient potpourris were kept moist, which often resulted in flowers rotting. Egyptians used to bury their dead with potpourri.

COOKING WITH ROSES

'She didn't like the eating part when there were people that made her shy and often wondered why you couldn't eat something poetical like violets or roses …'
—JAMES JOYCE (1882–1941), IRISH WRITER

Both rose flowers and rosehips are edible. The fragrant petals can be used in salads, as garnishes, or candied to make pastries. Rosehips taste quite tart, somewhat like cranberries, and are very high in vitamin C. If you want to experiment with recipes using the roses in your garden, be sure that the roses are free of pesticides. I usually just settle for ending my day with a nice cup of rosehip tea, made with teabags from the store, and enjoy my flowers as decorations.

There's a shop on Rose Avenue in Venice, California that specializes in rose petal ice cream.
'Anyone with a favourite ice cream mix (milk, cream, sugar, eggs) can make a rose petal ice cream. The trick is to add no vanilla extract. Just rose oil—or rosewater—or lots of rose petals (pesticide-free, obviously). The rose petals soaking in the mix base will impart a slight colour, so stick with roses of the same shade (we like pink petals only). We add crystallized rose petals when the ice cream is more than halfway frozen, so they keep their crystalline characteristic in the final product.'
—Robin Rose, proprietor of Robin Rose Ice Cream & Chocolate, Venice, CA

It is said that Shakespeare and his contemporaries ate rose petals in everything from tea to jellies. Roses are still commonly used in the Middle East for jams and flavoured syrups.

Interesting Facts about Rosehips

- Roses come from the same plant family as apples. Rosehips are the fruit of roses, and entire crops of roses are sometimes grown commercially for rosehips rather than flowers.

- Rosehips contain more vitamin C than oranges. The farther north of the equator that a rosehip is grown, the richer it will be in vitamin C.

- Rugosa roses are said to be the best for crops of rosehips, because they produce lots of edible pulp. They also have about 20 times more vitamin C than oranges.

You can eat rosehips fresh or dried, make them into syrup, preserves, jams and jellies, or add them to fruit pies.

- During World War II in England, when imported fresh citrus fruit was unavailable, the British government ordered that rosehips be gathered and processed into syrup, which was eaten to prevent scurvy.

> 'Yet no, not words, for they
> But half can tell love's feeling;
> Sweet flowers alone can say
> What passion fears revealing.'
> —Thomas Hood (1799–1845), *The Language of Flowers*

How romantic to have the petals of a flower known as Cupid's Pillow and Breath of Love, sprinkled over one's pillow. The Hastings House Inn on Saltspring Island, B.C., sprinkles rose petals on the pillows of honeymoon couples. The custom dates back to ancient Rome, when the rich and powerful slept on rose-filled cushions.

Jenni Lecuyer and Amy Leach, two of our staff members, make wonderful rose candles.

ATTAR-OF-ROSES, THE MOST PRECIOUS FRAGRANCE

On a wedding day long ago, according to legend, an Indian emperor and his new bride were walking along the canals that wound through the rose gardens. As they inhaled the fragrance of the flowers, they noticed an oily film around fallen petals on the surface of the water, and had the substance collected. This is the story of how attar-of-roses was discovered.

- Attar-of-roses is the essence of roses and the rarest, most costly fragrance in the world. It takes 180 pounds (82 kg) of roses—about 60,000 flowers—to make a single fluid ounce (28 ml) of rose oil.

- 'Joy' was introduced in 1935 as the world's most expensive perfume. It is a blend of two floral fragrances—jasmine and attar-of-roses—and remains a best-seller today.

- Damask roses have been cultivated since the first century BC for the production of this fragrant oil.

Rosaries were originally made with beads of rose petals.

Mme. Hardy is one of the best damask rose varieties.

Artist Laura Vickerson (right), of Calgary, Alberta, used 500,000 red rose petals, each skewered with a straight pin, in her artwork 'Velvet' (above). This work of art filled an entire room of a gallery, with two long carpets of rose petals descending from the walls and extending across the floor, covering the entire length of the room.

Great Rosarians

Prairie rose pioneer George Shewchuk, of Edmonton, Alberta, is truly a wealth of knowledge when it comes to growing roses. He has shared his years of experience through talks and publications, and has educated many gardeners.

'What's in a name? That which we call a rose,
by any other name would smell as sweet.'
—WILLIAM SHAKESPEARE (1564–1616),
ENGLISH PLAYWRIGHT AND POET

Below is a guide to the terms used in the individual variety descriptions (pages 85–158 and 167–241).

Official Colour • Rose varieties are given official colour classifications by the American Rose Society (ARS), which, in 1955, was designated the international registration authority for roses. Occasionally we disagree; for example, a variety officially described as 'red,' we might consider closer to 'pink.'

Flower Form • Flowers are described based on the number of petals. The opinions of other experts and rose growers may differ, but we consider the flowers as follows:

single—12 petals or less
semi-double—13–20 petals
double—20 or more petals.

single   *semi-double*

double

ARS rating • As well as assigning official colours, the ARS provides official ratings, which are an average of the ratings each rose receives based on nationwide performance. ARS members rate roses on a scale from 1 to 10. Ratings may change as varieties are re-evaluated every few years.

10.0—perfect
9.0–9.9—outstanding
8.0–8.9—excellent
7.0–7.9—good
6.0–6.9—fair
5.9 and lower—of questionable value

In ancient Persia, maidens attempted to bring back a wandering lover by boiling his shirt in rosewater and spices.

In some instances, a rose is too new to have an ARS rating, or there aren't enough reports to establish one. Don't rule a variety out just because it has a lower rating. Roses perform differently in various geographical areas. Just because a rose isn't of exhibition quality, doesn't mean it won't be an excellent garden rose.

Rose Organizations & Awards

There are a huge number of awards for roses, but keep in mind that a variety with no awards may still be the perfect choice for your garden. Awards such as AARS are given only to new rose varieties, and most often the entries are hybrid teas, grandifloras and floribundas. Testing is often carried out before a rose becomes available to the public, so an award can predate the rose's date of introduction.

AARS • Only roses introduced since the All-American Rose Selections committee was formed in 1938 are eligible for this award. Entries are grown at 24 test gardens in a wide range of climates across North America. Varieties are evaluated for two years by experts who rate each rose's disease resistance, form, hardiness, flowers and performance. Out of thousands of entries, only about 4 percent win awards.

ARS • The American Rose Society is the international registration authority for all roses. It provides a large number of awards in various categories, including Rose of the Year and the ARS Award of Excellence.

James Alexander Gamble Rose Fragrance Award • This is an award that, although it is available every year, has been given to only nine varieties since 1961. In order to qualify, roses must be heavily fragrant but also highly rated in other ways, too. There have been nine winners overall, including Tiffany (1962), Granada (1968), Fragrant Cloud (1970), Sunsprite (1979), and the most recent winner, Double Delight (1986). Since then, no variety has been considered worthy of this award.

World's Favourite Rose • Every three years, member rose societies from 31 countries around the world submit their choices for the top rose varieties to the World Federation of Rose Societies. The international votes are tabulated and a new World's Favourite Rose is named. Peace was the first variety to be named, in 1976.

Portland Gold Medal • Portland, Oregon, is the 'City of Roses,' and the International Rose Test Garden there has the most extensive display of roses in North America. The Portland Gold Medal is considered in some circles to be America's highest honour.

Other Awards • Many national rose societies provide gold medals or equivalent awards to outstanding varieties. The Bagatelle Gold Medal is from France, the Baden-Baden Gold Medal and ADR (Anerkannte Deutsche Rose) awards are from Germany, and the Royal National Rose Society awards are from England. The origins of other awards, such as the New Zealand Gold Star and Madrid Gold Medal, are obvious. Awards from the English and Irish rose societies are considered to be particularly significant, because of the extensive testing that is carried out.

Long ago in England, it was believed that if a maiden scattered red rose petals by the light of the moon on Midsummer's Eve and recited a chant as the clock struck 12, upon turning around she would see a vision of the man she was to marry.

FAVOURITE HARDY ROSES

'Some people are always grumbling
because the rose has thorns;

I am thankful that the thorns have roses.'
—ALPHONSE KARR (1808–90),
FRENCH WRITER AND EDITOR

The basic difference between hardy and tender roses is that hardy roses can survive cold winters without protection; tender roses cannot. Essentially, that is all you need to know. There are many different types and varieties of hardy roses to choose from, but the fundamental point is whether your rosebush is hardy or not.

Hardy roses are gaining in popularity, as more and more gardeners discover their carefree beauty. Because of their toughness, all hardy roses, generally, need little pruning and no winter protection, other than a good snowcover. Most also have good disease resistance.

There is a terrific blend of hardy shrub roses at the Royal Botanic Gardens in Hamilton, Ontario.

Explorer Series Roses

Canada's early explorers had to be pretty tough to survive the ordeals of surveying uncharted territories. In honour of these hardy men, Agriculture Canada created a series of equally tough roses. We were very excited when Explorer roses first came onto the scene, because this series offered a lot more choices of beautiful hardy roses. Explorer roses are derived from crosses of *Rosa rugosa* or *Rosa kordesii*. There are now 19 varieties within the series, ranging from low groundcovers to shrubs and climbers. All are amazingly hardy—even at temperatures as low as -40° F (-40° C).

❋ *The Explorer rose series has been called the world's most successful breeding program for winter–hardy roses. Although they were developed specifically for Canadian climates, these roses have since become very popular in other countries with harsh winters.*

Favourite Explorer Roses

Alexander Mackenzie
Captain Samuel Holland
Champlain
Charles Albanel
David Thompson
Frontenac
George Vancouver
Henry Hudson
Henry Kelsey
J.P. Connell

Jens Munk
John Cabot
John Davis
John Franklin
Louis Jolliet
Martin Frobisher
Quadra
Simon Fraser
William Baffin

Henry Hudson

Hardy Shrub Roses

This is a broad 'catch-all' category for roses that are able to survive harsh winters without protection, but do not fall into any particular class of roses. Hardy shrub roses include tall bushes, medium-sized shrubs, climbing roses, low-growing groundcovers and others that make excellent hedges.

Favourite Hardy Shrub Roses

Agnes
Alchymist
Blanc Double de Coubert
Dart's Dash
Double White Burnet
Euphrates
F.J. Grootendorst
Fimbriata
Frau Dagmar Hartopp
Frühlingsanfang
Frühlingsgold
Frühlingsmorgen
Hansa

Kakwa
Marie Bugnet
Max Graf
Nigel Hawthorne
Nozomi
Pavement Roses
Red Frau Dagmar
  Hartopp
Scabrosa
Schneezwerg
The Hunter
Thérèse Bugnet
Topaz Jewel

The Hunter

Old Garden Roses

Old garden roses are also known as antique roses, old-fashioned roses or simply old roses. They are known for their stunningly beautiful, fragrant flowers. 'Old garden roses' is a loose grouping that includes varieties that have been cultivated for one or more centuries—since before 1867, when the first modern roses were introduced. Old garden roses are survivors—tough and robust. Almost all old garden roses bloom once each season, but within that three- to four-week period they produce as many flowers as some other roses do throughout the entire season!

In my area of the country, where winter temperatures drop to -22° F (-30° C) or lower, old garden roses are 'borderline' hardy—more so than tender roses, but less so than other types of hardy roses. I mulch mine over in fall (see *What to Do in Fall, Winter & Spring* on page 61), just to be on the safe side. Without protection, they might survive, but then again, they might not; I want to be sure. In slightly warmer areas, such as southern Ontario, this step is not necessary.

Old garden roses like these Cabbage Roses usually have very full flowers and include some of the most fragrant roses.

Included in the category of old garden roses are varieties descended from the following species.

Rosa alba (Alba Rose, White Rose)—*Alba* is the Latin word for 'white'; alba roses have pale, fragrant flowers and blue-green foliage. In the Middle Ages, these roses were often used for medicinal purposes. Alba roses grow well in partial shade. Alba Maxima, Alba Semi-plena and Celestial are among my favourite varieties.

Rosa damascena (Damask Rose)—Damask roses have intense fragrance, and have been cultivated since the first century BC for attar-of-roses, the world's most expensive perfume. Autumn Damask, Botzaris and Mme. Hardy are damask roses.

Autumn Damask

Rosa gallica (Gallica Rose, French Rose)—The earliest-recorded roses grown in Europe are gallica roses. The most famous is *Rosa gallica officinalis*, the Apothecary's Rose. The flowers of gallica roses have the fragrance known as the true 'old rose' perfume. Alain Blanchard, Charles de Mills, Rosa Mundi and Superb Tuscan are gallica roses.

Favourite Old Garden Roses

Alain Blanchard	Charles de Mills
Alba Maxima	Hebe's Lip
Alba Semi-plena	Mme. Hardy
Autumn Damask	Reine des Violettes
Botzaris	Rosa Mundi
Cabbage Rose	Stanwell Perpetual
Celestial	Superb Tuscan

Parkland Series Roses

Parkland is another series of Canadian roses, developed at Agriculture Canada's Morden, Manitoba, Research Station. Parkland roses are bred specifically for prairie conditions, by crossing the native prairie rose (*Rosa arkansana*) with floribunda and hybrid tea roses. The result is small to medium-sized rosebushes with lots of double to semi-double flowers. Parkland roses are grown on their own roots and bloom on new wood. Most varieties bloom repeatedly until frost after an initial strong flush of flowers in early summer.

Morden Centennial

Favourite Parkland Roses

Adelaide Hoodless
Cuthbert Grant
Morden Amorette
Morden Blush
Morden Cardinette
Morden Centennial
Morden Fireglow
Morden Ruby
Winnipeg Parks

Great Rosarians

Agriculture Canada's Ian Ogilvie (right), along with Neville Arnold and Felicitas Svejda, played an integral part in the highly successful Explorer rose breeding program. Today many gardeners in Canada and around the world happily grow hardy Explorer roses.

Red-leaf Roses

Species Roses

Species roses are also known as 'wild roses'; it is from these roses that all other rose varieties are derived. Unlike most hybrid roses, which are grafted, species roses usually grow on their own rootstock and are extremely hardy. Species roses need little pruning, other than to remove any dead branches in spring, and they continue to produce more flowers even if you don't deadhead. Most species roses bloom once—except rugosas, which bloom repeatedly all summer. Species roses are tough shrubs that survive for years and years, and often thrive on old, abandoned farms, proof of their ability to withstand bugs, diseases and whatever nature throws at them.

Favourite Species Roses
Red Rugosa
Red-leaf Rose
Sweetbriar Rose
White Rugosa
Wingthorn Rose

The ability to bloom repeatedly is unusual for roses, although repeat-blooming has become common through the breeding of hybrid varieties. In the wild, there are just three species roses that bloom repeatedly: Rosa rugosa, R. fedtschenkoana and R. bracteata. Only the rugosa is winter-hardy where I live.

Rugosa Roses

Of the species roses, the rugosa rose (*Rosa rugosa*) is most commonly used in breeding other hardy rose varieties. Rugosa roses are renowned for their rugged hardiness and ability to tolerate not only extreme cold but also heat, drought and intense sunlight as well as partial shade. They have outstanding resistance to blackspot, and tolerate high levels of salt, whether from sea spray or de-icing salt, which makes them particularly good for growing near roadways.

As well, rugosa roses have a long blooming period and produce an outstanding display of colourful foliage and rosehips in fall. Many rugosa varieties also have fragrant flowers.

'Rugosa' means 'wrinkled' and refers to the look of the dark green leaves, which are distinctively crinkled, as if they had been folded up accordion-style.

FROZEN ROSE BOWL

Vicki Wilson designs spectacular iced rose bowls for dinner parties and special occasions. She says the frozen bowls are easy to make, and that they last quite a while before melting.

To make your own, use two mixing bowls, one a couple of inches smaller than the other. Line the bottom of the larger bowl with fresh rose flowers. Add about an inch of water and freeze. Once frozen, remove from freezer and place the smaller bowl inside the larger bowl. Place something like a jar of frozen sauce inside the smaller bowl to weight it. Arrange rose flowers between the two bowls, with some flowers facing in and some facing out. Fill the space between the two bowls with water, and freeze.

When you are ready to use your iced rose bowl, remove the two bowls. Set the iced rose bowl on top of a glass platter to catch any water, and fill with punch, fruit salad, shrimp salad or any other dish that you wish to keep cold.

Adelaide Hoodless

Parkland Series Rose

W hen visiting one of our supplier nurseries recently, the first thing that caught our nursery manager Shane Neufeld's eye was a spectacular 600-foot (180 m) hedge blazing with red flowers. As he drew nearer, he was astonished to find that this hedge was made up of about 150 bushy, glossy-leaved Adelaide Hoodless rosebushes. A single bush of Adelaide Hoodless bears well over 100 double, 2-inch (5 cm) flowers at one time, and it continues to bloom until fall frosts.

Official Colour • red
Form • double
Scent • slight
ARS rating • (—)
Height •
  5–6 feet (1.5–1.8 m)
Spread •
  5–6 feet (1.5–1.8 m)
Blooms •
  continuously from
  early summer to frost

HARDY

85

TIPS

* To promote repeat flowering, prune off finished flowers until a few weeks before the end of summer. From then on, let rosehips form, which signals the plant to prepare for winter. The red rosehips look decorative throughout fall and winter.

* This variety has good resistance to powdery mildew.

* For the best show of flowers, cut your rosebush back to about 2 to 3 feet (60–90 cm) and remove one or two of the oldest canes at ground level before the leaves unfold in spring.

* If you only prune off dead tips, bushes get quite tall, but stems may require support. One gardener ties his plant to a nearby upright blue juniper, resulting in an interesting effect with the contrasting red roses.

Adelaide Hoodless is named after the woman who founded the first Women's Institute of Canada in 1897.

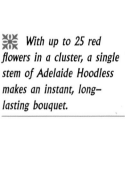

With up to 25 red flowers in a cluster, a single stem of Adelaide Hoodless makes an instant, long–lasting bouquet.

Hardy Shrub Rose

Agnes

Official Colour •
pale amber
Form • double
Scent • strong, fruity
ARS rating • 7.9
Height •
5–6 feet (1.5–1.8 m)
Spread •
5–6 feet (1.5–1.8 m)
Blooms • early summer

Agnes is a great shrub rose, with very fragrant, 3-inch (7.5 cm), double flowers in a lovely shade of buttercup yellow that softens with age to pale primrose or creamy white. The scent of these roses is absolutely wonderful. Agnes blooms abundantly in early summer, and occasionally again in late summer. This disease-resistant variety makes a great hedge, with compact form from top to bottom.

TIPS

* Avoid planting in windy sites. The delicate petals of these flowers are easily damaged by wind and heavy rains.

* To encourage a second flush of blooms, plant Agnes in the sunniest possible spot. Snip off finished flowers, and be sure to fertilize as recommended (see page 49).

* Agnes makes a wonderful hedge. Clip hard in the first year of planting to encourage bushiness, and then afterward clip only lightly to tidy your mature hedge. (See *Rose Hedges* on page 38.)

* This Canadian rose is a rugosa hybrid that was introduced in 1922. It won the Van Fleet Gold Medal in 1926.

Agnes is one of the few outstanding, hardy yellow roses.

Alain Blanchard

Old Garden Rose

A lain Blanchard is a lovely old rose, with very fragrant, 2 1/2- to 3-inch (6–7.5 cm), semi-double flowers. As flowers age, their crimson-purple petals become purple with red spots, which has a charming effect around golden stamens. Make the most of its invigorating fragrance by cutting flowers often for bouquets, or floating a single flower in a rosebowl placed in your favourite room.

Official Colour • mauve
Form • semi-double
Scent • very fragrant
ARS rating • 8.8
Height • 4 feet (l.2 m)
Spread • 4 feet (l.2 m)
Blooms • summer

HARDY

87

TIPS

* Alain Blanchard is a dense, vigorous shrub with thin, wiry, thorny stems that tend to flop over. If you don't like this look, plant the rosebush where its branches can easily be attached to a fence or pillar.

* Because of its growth habit, Alain Blanchard looks charming in a tall pot, which allows the rose's stems to trail over the sides. See page 43 for details on patio roses.

* Like most *Rosa gallica* cultivars, this variety tolerates partial shade and poor soil.

* Alain Blanchard is a French variety that was introduced in 1839.

 *Alain Blanchard has lots of stunning, highly fragrant flowers.*

HARDY

Official Colour • white
Form • very double
Scent • heavy
ARS rating • 8.3
Height •
  4–5 feet (1.2–1.5 m)
Spread • 4 feet (1.2 m)
Blooms • early to
  midsummer

Alba Maxima

When my daughter-in-law visited England, she admired the lovely white roses blooming in the countryside—very likely they were Alba Maxima. This long-lived rose often continues to thrive in old cottage gardens, long after residents and even the buildings are gone. Alba Maxima blooms profusely in early summer, with fragrant masses of rather informal-looking, $2^{1}/_{2}$- to 3-inch (6–7.5 cm) flowers that open blush pink in colour and fade to creamy white.

TIPS

* Alba Maxima is tolerant of partial shade and poor soil, but it performs best in rich soil and full sun.

* Two great features of this rose are that it is highly disease resistant, and it requires very little pruning.

* This rose dates back to at least 1867. It is believed to have been cultivated as early as the 1500s, although there is no hard proof. Alba Maxima is also known as The Jacobite Rose, Great White Double and simply Maxima.

Alba Maxima's fragrant, fully double flowers each have over 200 petals.

Alba Semi-plena

Old Garden Rose

Attar-of-roses is the rarest, most expensive perfume in the world, and Alba Semi-plena is one of the roses grown in Bulgaria for production of this fragrant oil. A rose dating back to the 1600s, Alba Semi-plena grows as a graceful, upright shrub with grey-green foliage. Its sweetly scented, 2 1/2- to 3-inch (6–7.5 cm) flowers have blush pink centres when they first open, and then fade to milky white. Abundant, large, red rosehips remain on branches throughout fall and winter.

Official Colour • white
Form • single
Scent • very strong
ARS rating • 8.6
Height •
  6–8 feet (1.8–2.4 m)
Spread •
  5–6 feet (1.5–1.8 m)
Blooms •
  early to midsummer

HARDY

89

TIPS

❋ Alba Semi-plena has very good tolerance of poor soil and shade, but more flowers are produced in full sun.

❋ To enjoy its fragrance indoors, snip off a flower or two to float in a rosebowl. If you want to add fragrance to potpourri (see page 69), collect flowers in mid-morning, after the sun has dried the dew from their petals.

❋ Alba Semi-plena is a *Rosa alba* (white rose) cultivar. It is sometimes confused with Alba Suaveolens, which is a different rose entirely.

❋ While Alba Semi-plena is considered a single rose, its flowers can have more than 12 petals.

❋ *Alba Semi–plena is one of the most fragrant roses.*

Hardy Shrub Rose climber

Official Colour •
   yellow, shaded orange,
   pink & red
Form • double
Scent • fragrant
ARS rating • 8.0
Height •
   5–6 feet (1.5–1.8 m)
Spread •
   5–6 feet (1.5–1.8 m)
Blooms • early summer

Alchymist is one of the best yellow–flowered hardy climbing roses.

Alchymist

Two types of roses often sell out before all others at our greenhouses: the yellow roses and the hardy climbers. Alchymist is both, so you can bet that these roses are snapped up as soon as they hit the sales floor. The 3-inch (7.5 cm) wide flowers are not pure yellow, but instead offer all the colours of a sunset, with blended shades of apricot, yellow, pink, red and egg-yolk orange. Add fragrance, large size and a high petal count for a truly outstanding rose.

TIPS

* The first flowers are pale, pastel shades; brighter-coloured flowers appear as the blooming season progresses.

* Though Alchymist blooms only once each season, it does so profusely. Later, the rosebush creates an attractive wall of very dense, glossy, bronze-green foliage, providing both beauty and privacy.

* Like most yellow roses, this variety is susceptible to blackspot. To help prevent this fungal disease, avoid wetting the foliage. Water at the base of the plant rather than from overhead.

* For the most flowers, do not cut this variety back. Leave it on its trellis over winter, and in spring, remove only dead canes and branch tips.

* The name 'Alchymist' means 'one who can change base metals into gold,' which may be a reference to the precious flowers. This variety was introduced in 1956.

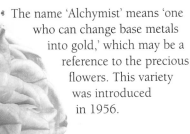

Alexander Mackenzie

If you like the look of hybrid tea roses, but don't want to be bothered with having to provide winter protection, Alexander Mackenzie is a dream come true. This large, shapely shrub is just covered with wave after wave of blooms throughout summer and into fall. The fragrant, 2 1/2- to 3-inch (6–7.5 cm) flowers have the classic cup-shape, and more petals per flower than many shrub roses, giving them a fuller appearance. With 6 to 12 flowers per cluster, you'll only need to cut one stem to make a bouquet!

Official Colour •
medium red
with lighter reverse
Form • double
Scent • fragrant
ARS rating • (—)
Height •
5–6 feet (1.5–1.8 m)
Spread •
4–5 ft (1.2–1.5 m)
Blooms •
repeatedly from early
summer to frost

TIPS

* Deadhead regularly. Removing finished flowers encourages more blooms.

* Although hardier than its fellow Explorers, John Franklin and Champlain, this rose does require some pruning of deadwood most springs.

* Alexander Mackenzie is highly resistant to blackspot and powdery mildew.

* This Canadian rose was introduced in 1985, and was named for the explorer famed for two expeditions. In 1789, Alexander Mackenzie was searching for the Pacific and inadvertently followed the Mackenzie River to its mouth—the Arctic Ocean. The second expedition in 1793 led him through northern Alberta and B.C. to the Pacific Ocean. He was knighted in 1802.

Alexander Mackenzie blooms profusely with big clusters of fragrant red flowers that look like the ones on hybrid teas!

Autumn Damask

Official Colour •
  medium pink
Form • double
Scent • heavy
ARS rating • 8.0
Height • 4 feet (1.2 m)
Spread • 4 feet (1.2 m)
Blooms • early and late
  summer to fall

Autumn Damask is a great rose. It blooms twice each season, marking the beginning and end of summer with its fragrant, silky pink, loosely double flowers. The foliage is grey-green and downy, and the flowers are 2 to 3 inches (5–7.5 cm) across. This variety, like all damask roses, is renowned for its intense fragrance. Most roses bloom the heaviest early in the season, but Autumn Damask blooms well later on, from late summer to fall. It is one of the oldest repeat-blooming roses.

TIPS

* Because of its lanky growth, plant Autumn Damask in a site where its long stems can easily be attached to a fence or pillar.

* This rose is susceptible to attacks of powdery mildew. To help prevent this disease, water in the morning rather than at night, and don't crowd the plants; good air circulation helps ward it off.

* This variety is one of the best roses for potpourri. Harvest flowers on a sunny day, after the moisture from rain or dew has dried from the petals.

* Autumn Damask dates back to 1819. It is also known as Rose des Quatre Saisons, Four Seasons Rose and Rose of Castille.

Damask roses have been used since the first century BC for making attar–of–roses, the world's most expensive perfume.

Blanc Double de Coubert

Blanc Double de Coubert has a superb fragrance: sweet, heady and very strong. This rose blooms abundantly in early to midsummer, and then less profusely until fall. The dazzling white, semi-double to double flowers are 2 $\frac{1}{2}$ to 3 inches (6–7.5 cm) across, with yellow stamens peeking out from the wavy petals. Blanc Double de Coubert is a tough, vigorous, upright, arching bush that makes an excellent hedge.

Official Colour • white
Form • semi-double
Scent • strong, sweet
ARS rating • 8.3
Height •
  4–6 feet (1.2–1.8 m)
Spread •
  4–5 feet (1.2–1.5 m)
Blooms • repeatedly
  from early summer
  to frost

TIPS

* Finished flowers cling to the rose branches and look quite messy. Regular deadheading will keep plants tidy and will encourage further blooming.

* Blanc Double de Coubert is a *Rosa rugosa* cultivar, with the rugosa's characteristic deep green, wrinkled, disease-resistant foliage and excellent fall colour.

* Large, round, bright scarlet rosehips are very decorative, and provide food for birds in fall and winter. This variety produces fewer rosehips than other rugosa cultivars.

* Blanc Double de Coubert is a very old French variety, introduced in 1892.

Blanc Double de Coubert is one of the whitest and most fragrant of roses, emitting a strong, sweet, heady scent even at night!

Botzaris

Old Garden Rose

HARDY

Official Colour • white
Form • double
Scent • strong
ARS rating • (—)
Height •
  3–4 feet (90–120 cm)
Spread •
  2–3 feet (60–90 cm)
Blooms • early summer

Botzaris puts everything it has into one stupendous show. The creamy white, highly fragrant flowers are 3 to 3 1/2 inches (7.5–8.5 cm) across, and very full. These flowers are 'quartered'—they have so many petals tightly packed together that each flower appears to be divided into four parts, rather than having petals encircling the centre. Botzaris is a damask rose, a type distinguished by its intense fragrance.

Tips

• Botzaris is quite tolerant of partial shade and poor soil, but it blooms best when grown in full sun and good soil.

• After the flowers finish, prune this shrub back by one-third to one-half to keep it compact. Botzaris blooms on old wood.

• I can't resist cutting these fragrant roses for bouquets or rosebowls. For over 2000 years, damask roses have been used to make attar-of-roses, the world's most expensive perfume.

• This variety dates back to 1856.

Botzaris has a powerful, enticing fragrance.

Cabbage Rose

L ike many other gardeners, I favour roses that bloom all summer, but the Cabbage Rose is an exception. Each year I look forward to those few weeks in early summer when the Cabbage Rose blooms, with its heady perfume and large, rounded, deep pink flowers, each up to 3 inches (7.5 cm) across, borne either one to a stem or in clusters. To make the most of the Cabbage Rose's enticingly sweet scent, plant it along a walkway, near a deck or under a window that is often open.

Official Colour •
  medium pink
Form • double
Scent • very strong,
  sweet
ARS rating • 7.9
Height •
  5–6 feet (1.5–1.8 m)
Spread •
  4–5 feet (1.2–1.5 m)
Blooms • early to
  midsummer

HARDY

95

TIPS

* Allow this large shrub lots of room when planting. It is wide-spreading, with rather lax, arching, thorny stems that often bow down under the weight of the flowers.

* The Cabbage Rose is susceptible to attacks of powdery mildew. See page 55.

* Unlike many roses, this variety tolerates poor soil and some shade, although plants will be less vigorous, not as bushy and have fewer flowers. Choose a site with full sun for at least half the day.

* The Cabbage Rose, which dates back to the early 1600s, is also known as *Rosa x centifolia*. Its round flowers look somewhat like cabbages. The name *centifolia* means '100 petals.'

When Cleopatra invited Mark Anthony to her bedroom, the floor was knee–deep in the fragrant petals of the Egyptian rose—more commonly known today as the Cabbage Rose.

Explorer Series Rose climber

HARDY

Official Colour •
    medium red
Form • double
Scent • light
ARS rating • (—)
Height •
    6–10 feet (1.8–3 m)
Spread •
    4–5 feet (1.2–1.5 m)
Blooms • continuously
    from early summer
    to frost

Captain Samuel Holland

Captain Samuel Holland is a gorgeous variety, with lots and lots of 3-inch (7.5 cm) flowers—more flowers than most other Explorer roses! Even young plants bloom profusely in nursery pots before they are planted into the garden. The flowers are sometimes borne one to a stem, and sometimes in clusters of up to 10. Although officially listed as red, they are actually fuchsia-pink. Regardless, expect a splendid display throughout the season.

TIPS

❋ Grow this rose as a large shrub or as a climber. For best blooming, plant in full sun.

❋ As well as being resistant to powdery mildew and blackspot, Captain Samuel Holland seems to be resistant to chewing insects that defoliate many other roses.

❋ Because it is sterile, this rose does not form rosehips.

❋ This variety is one of the newer Explorers, intro-duced in 1990. It is named after Captain Samuel Holland, a Royal Navy captain who surveyed Prince Edward Island and Cape Breton Island, and founded a system of township surveys in Lower and Upper Canada. He was appointed surveyor general of Quebec and of the northern district of North America in 1764.

Captain Samuel Holland makes an outstanding climber, with lots of flowers from June to frost.

Celestial

Celestial is a charming rose, with lots of cupped, uniform pale pink, semi-double flowers that open to expose golden stamens. This vigorous shrub has attractive grey-green foliage, and produces long, red rosehips in fall. What I like most about Celestial is its fragrance, which is strong and remarkably sweet. This is one of the oldest rose varieties.

Official Colour •
  light pink
Form • semi-double
Scent • very sweet
ARS rating • 8.6
Height • 4 feet (1.2 m)
Spread • 4 feet (1.2 m)
Blooms • early summer

TIPS

* Be careful when shopping for Celestial. There are three rose varieties that have this name: one is a Scots rose (*Rosa spinosissima*) hybrid and another is a hybrid tea rose, but our favourite Celestial is the white rose (*Rosa alba*) hybrid.

* Celestial has good resistance to powdery mildew and blackspot, but it can be susceptible to rust.

* Since Celestial blooms on old wood, don't prune too heavily—it results in few flowers.

* This Dutch variety dates back to the late 1700s. It is also known as Céleste.

Celestial has a very sweet scent and lovely shell-pink flowers.

Champlain

HARDY

98

Official Colour •
  dark red
Form • double
Scent • light
ARS rating • 8.1
Height •
  3–4 feet (90–120 cm)
Spread •
  3–4 feet (90–120 cm)
Blooms • continuously
  from early summer
  to frost

W ith its abundant clusters of $2^{1}/_{2}$- to 3-inch (6–7.5 cm), double flowers, Champlain is a beautiful rose, closely resembling a floribunda. The flowers are a true red, with velvety petals turning darker at the tips. Champlain has more flowers than foliage, and blooms profusely and continuously throughout summer and fall, until stopped by hard frosts. As an added bonus, this variety is unappealing to aphids and has excellent resistance to powdery mildew and blackspot.

TIPS

* Although Champlain usually requires a fair amount of spring pruning to remove deadwood, it bushes out quickly from its lower branches.

* This Canadian variety was introduced in 1982. It is named after Samuel de Champlain, a cartographer and explorer known as the 'Father of New France' for his role as founder and governor of the colony that once stretched from Quebec and Ontario south to Louisiana, until it fell under British rule in 1763.

Samuel de Champlain is credited with having been the first person to cultivate roses in North America. In the early 17th century, he brought roses from France to plant in his garden in Quebec.

Charles Albanel

Explorer Series Rose

Official Colour •
medium red
Form • semi-double
Scent • fragrant
ARS rating • (—)
Height •
1–2 feet (30–60 cm)
Spread •
2–3 feet (60–90 cm)
Blooms • repeatedly
from early summer
to frost

Charles Albanel is gaining in popularity as gardeners discover its suitability as a groundcover. Unlike many of the common hardy groundcover roses, Charles Albanel blooms throughout the season. This vigorous shrub provides lots of colour with fragrant clusters of 3-inch (7.5 cm), semi-double flowers. Though officially described as red, these flowers are really reddish purple. The foliage turns bright orange and yellow in fall.

TIPS

* Another option is to plant this dwarf shrub at the front of flowerbeds. A row of three interspersed amongst bedding plants or perennials is very effective.

* Finished flowers tend to cling to the branches. Regular deadheading keeps plants tidy and promotes further blooming.

* Stop deadheading a few weeks before the end of summer, to allow the very attractive, large, orange-red rosehips to form. This flower is a *Rosa rugosa* cultivar, with wrinkled foliage, great fall colour and outstanding resistance to blackspot and powdery mildew.

* This Canadian rose was introduced in 1982. It was named after Father Charles Albanel, a Jesuit priest, missionary and explorer who, in 1672, was likely the first non-native to reach Hudson Bay by land.

Charles Albanel is the smallest rosebush in the Explorer series, and makes an outstanding groundcover, blooming repeatedly and profusely well into fall.

Old Garden Rose

Official Colour • mauve
Form • double
Scent • strong 'old rose' fragrance
ARS rating • 8.2
Height •
 4–5 feet (1.2–1.5 m)
Spread •
 3 ¹/₂–4 feet (1–1.2 m)
Blooms • late spring to early summer

Charles de Mills

Charles de Mills is a truly stunning rose, with whipped-up whirls of petals forming fragrant flowers up to 4 ¹/₂ inches (11 cm) across, usually in clusters of four. The flowers are flat, with petals that seem sliced-off, but the effect is pleasing. Although officially described as mauve, I find the colour is more a deep, rich purple-crimson, fading to maroon and purple as flowers age. This variety blooms longer than most old garden roses.

TIPS

* To enjoy the intense perfume, plant Charles de Mills near a garden seat or under a window that is often open.

* This variety has great disease resistance and its long, arching stems have few thorns.

* Charles de Mills tolerates partial shade and poor soil, but when grown under ideal conditions, this shrub will be larger with more flowers.

* This stunning *Rosa gallica* hybrid dates back to the early 1800s. It originates from France, and is also known as Bizarre Triomphante.

✳ *Charles de Mills is one of the largest–flowered and most spectacular old garden roses!*

Cuthbert Grant

Parkland Series Rose

Cuthbert Grant has large, deep crimson, velvety-petalled flowers, about 4 inches (10 cm) across. They are borne in clusters of three to six, resulting in a splendid display of sumptuous colour. This variety has luxuriant, glossy foliage with excellent resistance to blackspot and powdery mildew. Cuthbert Grant is a vigorous, upright shrub with tight rosebuds like the ones on a hybrid tea rose, and with the ability to quickly bounce back after severe winters.

Official Colour • red
Form • semi-double
Scent • light
ARS rating • (—)
Height •
  3–4 feet (90–120 cm)
Spread •
  3–4 feet (90–120 cm)
Blooms • repeatedly
  from early summer to
  frost

TIPS

* Remove the entire cluster after blooming to promote further flowering. Usually, most flowers are produced at the beginning and end of summer.

Cuthbert Grant has an impressive abundance of beautiful, fragrant, velvety, crimson flowers.

* Cuthbert Grant is a Canadian rose named after a Northwest Company fur trader who was a founder of the Métis Nation. Grant led the Métis to victory at Seven Oaks, where 21 Selkirk settlers were killed in 1816.

* This variety was introduced in 1967, and was chosen as Manitoba's Centennial Rose that year. It received the Award of Merit in 1970 from the Western Canadian Society for Horticulture.

Dart's Dash

Hardy Shrub Rose

Official Colour •
  medium purple-
  crimson
Form • semi-double
Scent • strong, sweet
ARS rating • (—)
Height •
  3 1/2–4 feet (1–1.2 m)
Spread •
  3 1/2–4 feet (1–1.2 m)
Blooms • repeatedly
  from early summer
  to frost

Dart's Dash is like a smaller version of Hansa, one of the best-known shrub roses. Its 3- to 4-inch (7.5–10 cm) wide flowers are the same mauve-red colour, and have a heavy, sweet perfume. Dart's Dash blooms repeatedly all summer, and continues until after the first light fall frosts, often producing flowers alongside its immense red-orange rosehips. The foliage is very dense, and turns bright orange in fall.

Tips

* With its thick foliage and even size, this rose makes an outstanding hedge or groundcover.

* If you want to harvest rosehips, Dart's Dash is a great variety to grow. Its red-orange hips are large, very fleshy and produced abundantly.

* The date that this Dutch variety was introduced is unknown. It is a *Rosa rugosa* cultivar with attractive, dark green, very wrinkled, disease-resistant foliage.

Dart's Dash has impressive, large flowers with a strong, sweet perfume.

David Thompson

Every year for the past seven years our nursery manager Shane Neufeld gave his mother a rosebush for Mother's Day, and out of the 250 varieties that we carry, this rose was his favourite choice. David Thompson blooms in profuse waves from July to frost, with large fragrant flowers about 3 inches (7.5 cm) across. Though its official colour designation is medium red, the flowers are really closer to deep fuchsia in colour. This variety forms a nice compact bush and is one of the least thorny Explorers.

Official Colour • medium red
Form • double
Scent • fragrant
ARS rating • (—)
Height •
  3–4 feet (90–120 cm)
Spread •
  4–5 feet (1.2–1.5 m)
Blooms • repeatedly from early summer to frost

TIPS

* Because this variety is sensitive to alkaline soil, it's a good idea to add lots of peat moss when planting.

David Thompson blooms abundantly all summer with large, fragrant flowers.

* David Thompson is a *Rosa rugosa* cultivar, with the rugosa's characteristic wrinkled foliage and high resistance to blackspot and powdery mildew. Unlike most rugosas, however, this variety does not form rosehips.

* This Canadian variety was introduced in 1979. Its namesake, David Thompson, was a famous Canadian fur trader, explorer, surveyor and mapmaker. Thompson was apprenticed to the Hudson's Bay Company in 1784, and in the years that followed, his maps were the first to detail the western territories (now Manitoba, Saskatchewan and Alberta).

Official Colour • white
Form • double
Scent • heavy
ARS rating • (—)
Height • 3 feet (90 cm)
Spread • 3 feet (90 cm)
Blooms • late spring

Double White Burnet

The first time that I saw Double White Burnet, I was surprised at the size of its leaves—they are as tiny as mouse ears! Overall, however, the foliage is thick and forms a bushy, tidy shrub that turns orange and yellow in fall. The pure white, rounded flowers are 2 to 3 inches (5–7.5 cm) across, and look immense against the tiny leaves. Double White Burnet blooms early and profusely, emitting a powerful, entrancing perfume similar to that of lily-of-the-valley.

TIPS

Double White Burnet is one of the smaller hardy roses, and one of the first roses to bloom, with a profusion of very fragrant flowers in late spring.

* Plant this rose in a mixed flowerbed or as a groundcover. It also makes a nice, tidy, low hedge.

* Double White Burnet grows well in sun or partial shade.

* Don't deadhead this variety. It forms very attractive, small, round rosehips that turn dark chocolate-brown in late summer.

* This variety is an enduring rose that has been cultivated since the early 19th century. It is a *Rosa spinosissima* (Scots rose) hybrid, with prickly branches, and it is sometimes called Double Scots White or Scotch Double White.

Euphrates

O ne of the most extraordinary roses I have ever seen is a scarlet-eyed hybrid that we discovered about four years ago: Euphrates. Some rose varieties have central splotches or 'eyes' in the flowers, but with only a light contrast between eyes and petals. Euphrates is unusual in that each of its 2- to 2 1/2-inch flowers have a very pronounced, deep scarlet-pink eye, contrasting with outer petals that begin rose-salmon and later fade to soft peach. With flowers in clusters of three to nine, the effect is a stunning palette of pastel hues. Other than its partner, Nigel Hawthorne (see page 135), few other roses have darker eyes.

Official Colour • pale salmon with red eye
Form • single
Scent • none
ARS rating • (—)
Height • 2–2 1/2 feet (60–75 cm)
Spread • 3–3 1/2 feet (90–105 cm)
Blooms • late spring to early summer

TIPS

* This variety is a low-growing bush with tiny leaves and long, arching branches that trail along the ground. Euphrates makes a charming groundcover.

* Unlike most roses, this variety does well in sun or shade. It is sometimes subject to blackspot.

* Euphrates is a remarkably tough rose, able to withstand temperatures at both extremes. It thrives in hot, sunny areas of the garden but needs little protection, other than a good snowcover, to survive winter unscathed.

* This variety was introduced in 1986, but the supply remains limited because it is harder to propagate than others and is in high demand. Euphrates is named after one of the most important rivers in the Middle East.

Euphrates is a rare rose that produces a spectacular show of unusual, scarlet–eyed flowers.

Official Colour •
  bright red
Form • double
Scent • little to none
ARS rating • 7.7
Height •
  5–6 feet (1.5–1.8 m)
Spread •
  4–5 feet (1.2–1.5 m)
Blooms • continuously
  from early summer
  to frost

We tell new staff at the greenhouses that when customers ask for 'the carnation rose,' F.J. Grootendorst is usually the one they mean. With its fringed petals and large, tight sprays of bright red, 1 1/2-inch (3.5 cm), double flowers, this rose does look remarkably like a carnation. One of its best features is that, with up to 20 flowers in a single spray, one stem is all you need to cut for an instant bouquet!

TIPS

* F.J. Grootendorst performs admirably in sites that receive sun for only half the day.

* With its small, thick, leathery, lime-green leaves, profuse flowers and strong, vigorous growth habit, this rose makes a very showy informal hedge. The stems are quite thorny.

* Despite its delicate-looking flowers, this variety is one tough rosebush. It has excellent disease resistance and withstands drought, poor or salty soil and extreme cold without any problem at all.

* This Dutch rose was introduced in 1918. Since then, other varieties have been added, including Pink Grootendorst, which has soft pink, double roses, and Grootendorst Supreme, which has double roses in a darker shade of red. Grootendorst Red is just another name for F.J. Grootendorst.

F.J. Grootendorst blooms long and heavily, with unique flowers that have serrated petals like the ones on carnations.

Fimbriata

Fimbriata is sometimes also called 'the carnation rose,' because of the look of its flowers. These frilly flowers are about 2 to 2 1/2 inches (5–6 cm) across, with fringed, pale pink petals blushed in white and a powerful fragrance. Fimbriata blooms in profusion, almost continuously throughout summer until fall frost. This variety should be planted in a prominent site where it is convenient for you to 'stop and smell the roses.'

Official Colour •
 soft pink
Form • double
Scent • very fragrant
ARS rating • (—)
Height •
 3 1/2–4 feet (1–1.2 m)
Spread •
 3 1/2–4 feet (1–1.2 m)
Blooms • repeatedly
 from early summer
 to frost

TIPS

* With its dense, bright green foliage and long blooming period, Fimbriata makes an excellent hedge. These rosebushes grow as wide as they are tall.

* Fimbriata's leaves turn bright orange in fall. It is a *Rosa rugosa* cultivar, with the usual extreme hardiness but without the typical look of rugosa flowers. Fimbriata also has fewer rosehips and only slightly crinkled leaves.

* This rose is a very old French variety, introduced in 1891. Other names are Phoebe's Frilled Pink and Dianthiflora, both referring to the look of the flowers.

Fimbriata produces lots of very fragrant, charming, little flowers with fringed petals.

Frau Dagmar Hartopp

Hardy Shrub Rose

HARDY

108

Official Colour •
   silvery pink
Form • single
Scent • strong, clove-like
ARS rating • 8.5
Height • 2–3 feet
   (60–90 cm)
Spread • 4–5 feet
   (1.2–1.5 m)
Blooms • repeatedly
   from early summer
   to frost

Frau Dagmar Hartopp is an impressive rose, with silky-petalled, silvery-pink flowers that shimmer in sunlight. These highly perfumed, poppy-like flowers are large, from 3 to 3 ¹/₂ inches (7.5–8.5 cm) across, and cupped like a wine glass around creamy yellow stamens. This variety blooms until stopped by fall frost, with the greatest profusion of flowers in early and late summer. During fall, it is one of the most impressive roses: it has large red rosehips, which look like cherry tomatoes, and glossy foliage, which changes from green to purple-red to deep golden-yellow brushed with copper.

TIPS

* Most roses need full sun—eight or more hours of sunlight every day—but Frau Dagmar Hartopp does well even with shade for half the day.

* Frau Dagmar Hartopp makes an excellent ground-cover. When planted under a window, its thorny stems create a formidable barrier against intruders.

* This variety is very vigorous and highly resistant to the two most common rose diseases: blackspot and powdery mildew.

* When shopping for this rose, you may find it listed by a slightly different name. Frau Dagmar Hartopp is also known as Frau Dagmar Hastrup, Fru Dagmar Hastrup and Fru Dagmar Hartopp. This Danish variety was introduced in 1914.

Frau Dagmar Hartopp has flowers of an unusual silvery-pink colour and very large, cherry tomato–like rosehips.

Frontenac

Frontenac puts on a spectacular show in early summer, becoming completely covered with small clusters of large, deep pink flowers. This variety has a long blooming period, continuing to produce flowers, although less profusely, until at least the end of September. These fragrant flowers are 3 1/2 inches (8.5 cm) across, and show off nicely against very healthy, deep green, glossy foliage.

Official Colour •
  deep pink
Form • double
Scent • fragrant
ARS rating • (—)
Height • 2 1/2–3 feet
  (75–90 cm)
Spread • 2 1/2–3 feet
  (75–90 cm)
Blooms • continuously
  from early summer
  to frost

TIPS

* Plant this upright shrub in mixed flowerbeds for a showy display throughout summer. A row of these roses makes a lovely border or low hedge.

* Frontenac is very hardy and requires only minimal pruning in spring. It is highly resistant to black-spot and powdery mildew.

* This variety is one of the latest Explorer roses, introduced in 1992. It was named after Louis de Buade, Comte de Frontenac, a governor general of New France during the late 1600s. (New France was a French colony ranging from Quebec and Ontario south to Louisiana, from the early 16th century until 1763.)

Frontenac has fragrant clusters of deep pink flowers all summer and well into fall.

Frühlingsanfang

Official Colour •
  ivory white
Form • single
Scent • heavy
ARS rating • 7.3
Height •
  9–10 feet (2.7–3 m)
Spread •
  6–7 feet (1.8–2 m)
Blooms • early summer

✻ *Frühlingsanfang is one of the largest hardy shrub roses, with big flowers and a powerful fragrance.*

Frühlingsanfang is a fast-growing rose, reaching its impressive mature size within just six years. The ivory flowers are very fragrant and big—up to 4 inches (10 cm) across—with decorative stamens. Grow it near a walkway, so you can enjoy its scent. Once it becomes large enough to hold its own, plant a flowering vine like clematis or canary bird vine to climb through the branches. Frühlingsanfang blooms profusely in early summer.

TIPS

* Frühlingsanfang tolerates poor soil and grows well even with shade for half the day.

* Don't deadhead this rose. In fall, it forms very large, decorative rosehips in an uncommon maroon colour.

* Despite its name, which in German means 'the beginning of spring,' Frühlingsanfang blooms later and longer than the other 'Frühlings' roses. This variety was introduced in 1950.

Frühlingsgold

Good, hardy, yellow climbing roses are hard to come by, so we were delighted to discover Frühlingsgold. This stunning rose blooms early, with a profusion of richly scented, 3-inch (7.5 cm) flowers that begin rich golden-yellow in colour and soften to pale primrose. Its vigorous branches are very spiny. Plant it against a trellis near a walkway or deck to make the most of its delicious perfume.

Hardy Shrub Rose climber

HARDY
III

Official Colour •
    creamy yellow
Form • single
Scent • heavy
ARS rating • 7.6
Height •
    5–7 feet (1.5–2 m)
Spread •
    5–7 feet (1.5–2 m)
Blooms • late spring
    to early summer

TIPS

* Leave Frühlingsgold on its trellis over winter, and remove any dead tips or branches in spring.

* If you like, grow Frühlingsgold as a large, bushy shrub instead of a climber. Several bushes planted 5 to 6 feet (1.5–1.8 m) apart make an excellent, informal hedge.

* This variety has good resistance to powdery mildew, but like most yellow roses, it can be subject to blackspot. To help prevent this fungal disease, avoid wetting the foliage. Water at the base of the plant rather than from overhead.

* Frühlingsgold is a German variety that was introduced in 1937. Its name means 'spring gold,' and you may find it listed under either of these names.

Frühlingsgold is one of the best hardy, yellow climbing roses!

Frühlingsmorgen

Hardy Shrub Rose
climber

Official Colour •
cherry pink with
soft yellow centre
Form • single
Scent • fragrant
ARS rating • 7.5
Height •
5–6 feet (1.5–1.8 m)
Spread •
3 1/2–4 feet (1–1.2 m)
Blooms • late spring to
early summer

*Frühlingsmorgen is one of
the most beautiful single roses.*

The arching stems of Frühlingsmorgen are covered in showers of pink and cream, 2 1/2-inch (6 cm) flowers in late spring to early summer, and occasionally again in late summer. This rose is very pretty, with uncommon flowers and fragrance. Unlike most roses, which have yellow stamens, Frühlingsmorgen has showy, maroon stamens that are surrounded by soft-hued petals. These petals brighten to yellow at the flower's centre, forming a prominent eye. The floral fragrance is unusual, and reminds me of the sweet smell of freshly cut hay.

TIPS

* Most roses need full sun—eight or more hours of direct sunlight every day—but this variety does well even with shade for half the day. It also tolerates poor soil.

* To grow this rose as a climber, attach its arching stems to a trellis. Alternatively, allow it to grow as a large shrub.

* Once Frühlingsmorgen is close to mature size, you can plant a later-blooming clematis vine to clamber through its branches and prolong the season of interest. Very large, red rosehips provide decoration in fall.

* Frühlingsmorgen is a German variety that was introduced in 1942. It blooms earlier than most roses, and its name means 'spring morning.'

George Vancouver

George Vancouver is a nice, compact rosebush with an incredible number of flowers. It blooms in early summer, and, with brief breaks, repeats through summer until at least late September. Often you will find just one 2 1/2-inch (6 cm) flower per stem, but usually the flowers form in clusters of up to six. In fall, hundreds of bright red rosehips decorate the branches. With its compact size and abundant blooms, this rose is ideal for planting in mixed flowerbeds or small gardens.

Official Colour •
  medium red
Form • double
Scent • light
ARS rating • (—)
Height • 2–2 1/2 feet
  (60–75 cm)
Spread • 2–2 1/2 feet
  (60–75 cm)
Blooms • repeatedly
  from early summer
  to frost

TIPS

* Although petals fall cleanly from the finished flowers, regular deadheading will encourage further blooming. Remove the entire cluster after flowering.

* George Vancouver is highly resistant to blackspot and powdery mildew.

* This variety was introduced in 1994, in honour of the Victoria Commonwealth Games. It is named for the naval officer who explored the B.C. coast-line in the late 1700s and later confirmed the existence of a Northwest Passage from the Pacific to the Atlantic with his survey.

George Vancouver produces well over 100 flowers at one time!

Hansa

Official Colour •
  mauve-red
Form • double
Scent • strong clove
  fragrance
ARS rating • 8.3
Height •
  4–5 feet (1.2–1.5 m)
Spread •
  5–6 feet (1.5–1.8 m)
Blooms • repeatedly,
  all summer

On country drives, Ted and I sometimes pass old abandoned farmhouses where, in the midst of overgrown shrubs, knee-high grass and dilapidated buildings, more than once we have spotted a huge Hansa bush, blooming profusely and thriving all on its own, long after the people who once tended it last set foot on the property. This carefree rose blooms all summer, with large, fragrant, fuchsia-red flowers, and then puts on a showy display in fall, with orange leaves and large, gleaming red rosehips, which remain on branches into winter.

TIPS

* Hansa thrives even in silty clay or sandy soil, but doesn't do well in alkaline soil. To prevent chlorosis (pale, unhealthy leaves), mix in lots of peat moss before planting.

* These upright, arching shrubs make excellent hedges. See *Rose Hedges* on page 38.

* Hansa's flower production declines as its canes age. For the best floral show, any canes older than five years should be removed at the soil line in late fall, or early spring before leaves appear. If you want to keep the bush shorter, lightly prune the tips after the first show of flowers.

* This variety is one of the longest-lived and toughest roses, able to take pretty much whatever nature throws at it. Hansa rarely shows winter damage, even in the coldest areas.

Hansa is one of the best all-round rugosa roses, noted for its large, vibrant, double flowers, intense fragrance and unfailing ability to bloom repeatedly.

Hebe's Lip

Old Garden Rose

I n late spring to early summer, Hebe's Lip is showered
in flowers. Fat, creamy white, pointed rosebuds tipped
in red open to lightly scented, cupped flowers, each
3 inches (7.5 cm) across, with showy golden stamens and
petals edged in red to pink. In Greek mythology, Hebe
was the goddess of youth, daughter of Hera and Zeus.
Hebe's Lip is a cross between a damask rose and the
Sweetbriar Rose, and has the latter's characteristic, fresh
green, fragrant foliage.

Official Colour • white
Form • semi-double
Scent • light
ARS rating • 7.3
Height •
  4 feet (1.2 m)
Spread •
  4–5 feet (1.2–1.5 m)
Blooms • early summer

HARDY

115

TIPS

* Like the Sweetbriar Rose, the branches of Hebe's
Lip are very thorny. Foliage fragrance is strongest
at the tips of the shoots.

* This variety dates back to 1846, and is also known
as Rubrotincta and Reine Blanche.

* Because Hebe's Lip blooms on old wood, prune
as little as possible in spring, so the upcoming
show of flowers won't be diminished. Leave major
pruning until after blooming has finished.

* Although the Sweetbriar Rose is hardy, Hebe's Lip
is not. Provide this variety with winter protection
as recommended on page 62.

*Hebe's Lip has fragrant
foliage, with a sweet apple scent
that is strongest after a rainfall,
or whenever the air is damp.*

Henry Hudson

HARDY

116

Official Colour • white
Form • double
Scent • strong,
  spicy-clove
ARS rating • 9.1
Height • 1 1/2–2 feet
  (45–60 cm)
Spread • 3–4 feet
  (90–120 cm)
Blooms • repeatedly
  from early summer
  to frost

Henry Hudson's flowers are like apple-blossoms: pink flowerbuds open to sparkling white flowers. These richly scented roses are 2 1/2 inches (6 cm) across, shown off to great advantage against thick, deep green foliage. Henry Hudson blooms profusely, with wave after wave of showy flowers from early summer to frost. In cool weather, flowers are tinged in pink. With its low, spreading, dense growth, this rose makes an outstanding groundcover.

TIPS

* Finished flowers tend to cling to this bush. Deadhead regularly until a few weeks before the end of summer to keep plants tidy and encourage further blooming.

* Henry Hudson is a *Rosa rugosa* cultivar, and has the usual distinctive, wrinkled, disease-free foliage. This variety does not produce rosehips.

* This rose was introduced in 1976. It is named after the explorer who in 1610 became the first known European to sail into Hudson Bay. After Henry Hudson failed to find a Northwest Passage, his mutinous crew set him adrift with his son and seven others. None of them was ever seen again.

Henry Kelsey

Explorer Series Rose climber

Who can resist a climbing rose that is absolutely covered in fragrant, red, 2 1/2- to 3 1/2-inch (6–8 cm), double flowers throughout summer? Henry Kelsey blooms in profusion, providing an impressive show against a trellis or fence. Have faith in this variety's potential, because, like many other types of plants, these roses often look rather scraggly in nursery pots. Believe me! Time and again, I reassure customers at our greenhouses that those long lax canes undergo a transformation once this rose is planted in your garden and affixed to a trellis. Henry Kelsey soon bushes out to become one of the showiest plants in your garden.

Official Colour • medium red
Form • double
Scent • spicy
ARS rating • (—)
Height • 7–8 feet (2.1–2.4 m)
Spread • 6–8 feet (1.8–2.4 m)
Blooms • repeatedly from early summer to frost

Tips

* Have patience—young plants tend to have more flowers than leaves; Henry Kelsey may not reach its full potential until a year or two after planting.

* I like this rose best as a climber, but some gardeners choose to grow it as a wide-spreading shrub. Either way, its long, trailing branches bloom prolifically, with 9 to 18 flowers in each cluster.

* Henry Kelsey has good resistance to powdery mildew.

* For best results, grow this variety in a sheltered location, against the south or west wall of a heated building. Ensure that as much of the canes as possible are well-covered in snow throughout winter.

* Henry Kelsey was introduced in 1984. Its namesake explorer served the Hudson's Bay Company for 40 years, and journeyed across the vast Prairies in 1690–92.

J.P. Connell

Official Colour • yellow
Form • double
Scent • 'tea rose'
fragrance
ARS rating • (—)
Height •
2–3 feet (60–90 cm)
Spread •
2–3 feet (60–90 cm)
Blooms • repeatedly
from early summer
to frost

A t our greenhouses, J.P. Connell is the fastest-selling Explorer rose. Yellow roses are always in high demand, especially hardy varieties that bloom all summer. Since J.P. Connell also has beautiful, fragrant flowers and is small enough to complement any flowerbed, it's small wonder that gardeners snap up these thornless shrubs as soon as they see them. The double, 3- to 3¹/₂-inch (7.5-8.5 cm) flowers are lemon-yellow when they first open, with high centres like a hybrid tea. The petals then fall back to expose stamens, and fade to a lovely, soft buttery-cream colour.

TIPS

• Have patience with new roses. J.P. Connell blooms sparsley for the first year or two after planting. In later years, it blooms better, with more abundant, larger flowers and stronger colour than initially.

• J.P. Connell has good resistance to powdery mildew, and better resistance to blackspot than most yellow roses. It can, however, still be susceptible, so avoid wetting the foliage: water at the base of the plant rather than from overhead.

• This variety was introduced in 1987. There is some debate about whether or not this rose is a true Explorer. We count it within the ranks of this series because it originated from the same breeding program in Ottawa. It was named after the retired federal civil servant, a rose enthusiast who worked for Agriculture Canada.

J.P. Connell blooms one to a stem or in clusters of three to eight, in wave after wave throughout the season. Expect the most flowers in early and late summer.

Jens Munk

Jens Munk starts and ends the summer with a bang, producing two profuse flushes of fragrant, bright pink flowers. In between, it blooms with fewer flowers, and then continues to bloom after most other roses are finished, bearing both flowers and bright red rosehips at the same time. Its double flowers are almost 3 inches (7.5 cm) across, and are often marked with a striking white streak. Young plants quickly become established, bushing out and blooming well, soon after planting.

Official Colour • medium pink
Form • double
Scent • spicy
ARS rating • 8.4
Height •
  4–5 feet (1.2–1.5 m)
Spread •
  5–6 feet (1.5–1.8 m)
Blooms • repeatedly from early summer to frost

HARDY

119

TIPS

* Jens Munk makes a dense and colourful, though prickly, hedge. For details on growing rose hedges, see page 38.

* Expect a showy display in fall, with yellow-orange leaves. The large, gleaming red rosehips remain on branches into winter.

* Jens Munk is a *Rosa rugosa* cultivar with the rugosa's distinctive, crinkled foliage and outstanding resistance to blackspot and powdery mildew.

* This variety became the second rose in the Explorer series, when it was introduced in 1974. It is named after the Norwegian explorer Jens Munk, who in 1619, sailed in search of a Northwest Passage. He was unsuccessful: 61 of his men died of scurvy, and he and two survivors returned home the following year.

Jens Munk is one of the hardiest roses for extremely cold areas.

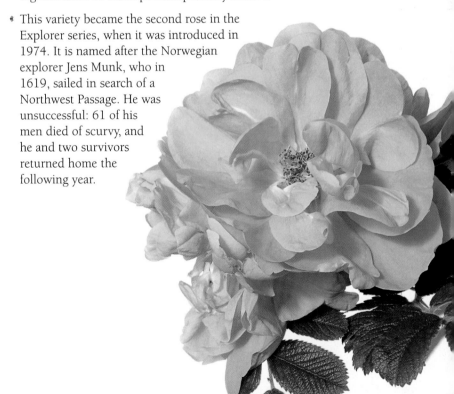

John Cabot

Official Colour •
medium red
Form • double
Scent • fragrant
ARS rating • 8.2
Height •
8–10 feet (2.4–3 m)
Spread •
5–7 feet (1.5–2 m)
Blooms • repeatedly
from early summer
to frost

A lot of proud parents show off snapshots of the kids, but the photos I see most often are of people's prized flowers. Recently, a woman brought to the greenhouses some pictures her husband had taken of her Explorer climbing roses. This couple were thrilled with their roses—John Cabot and fellow Explorer William Baffin—which were absolutely covered with flowers and, three years after planting, towered above the front doorway. John Cabot blooms most heavily in the early summer months, and keeps on blooming into fall.

Tips

* Although officially described as red, these 2 ½-inch (6 cm) flowers actually range in colour from deep orchid-pink to red-purple.

* As an alternative to a climber, John Cabot may be allowed to grow into a large shrub. When not affixed to a trellis, its long canes arch outward, resulting in a height of about 5 to 6 feet (1.5–1.8 m) and a spread of 8 to 10 feet (2.4–3 m).

* This variety has good resistance to both powdery mildew and blackspot.

* Introduced in 1978, John Cabot was the first climbing rose in the Explorer series, and has since become one of the best-known Canadian roses. Its namesake explorer, the Anglo-Italian navigator John Cabot, made the first recorded North American landing since the Norse voyages, arriving in Newfoundland in 1497 under the authority of Henry VII. This voyage is often pointed to as the basis for the English claim to North America.

John Cabot is an irresistible climbing rose, with waves of fragrant flowers that brighten gardens until fall frost.

John Davis

John Davis is one of the most popular climbing roses, with its profuse, showy, 3 1/2-inch (8.5 cm) flowers and deep red, trailing branches. This variety was one of the first Explorer roses that we sold at our greenhouses, and a decade later it continues to be a best-seller. Not only is it very hardy, disease-free and undemanding, it is also one of the longest-blooming roses. John Davis blooms non-stop all season, with up to 17 pure pink, full, double flowers in a single cluster.

TIPS

* As an alternative to growing John Davis on a trellis, allow this rose to ramble along a fence. With its trailing stems, lush, healthy foliage and profuse flowers, John Davis puts on a splendid display.

* Another option is to grow this variety unchecked, allowing it to spread and form a large, arching bush.

* John Davis is highly resistant to both blackspot and powdery mildew.

* Introduced in 1986, this variety is named after explorer John Davis, who searched for a Northwest Passage between the years 1585–87. His name was given to the passage between Baffin Island and Greenland: Davis Strait.

Explorer Series Rose climber

Official Colour •
   medium pink
Form • double
Scent • spicy
ARS rating • 8.5
Height •
   5–6 feet (1.5–1.8 m)
Spread •
   4–6 feet (1.2–1.8 m)
Blooms • continuously
   from early summer
   to frost

 Few climbing roses can match John Davis for its hardiness, profusion of charming flowers and long blooming period.

John Franklin

Official Colour •
medium red
Form • double
Scent • light
ARS rating • (—)
Height • 3–4 feet
(90–120 cm)
Spread • 3–3 ½ feet
(90–105 cm)
Blooms • continuously
from early summer
to frost

*John Franklin blooms
profusely and is an ideal size
for planting in borders and
small gardens.*

I f you're looking for a red rosebush to tuck into a
flowerbed, John Franklin is perfect. This compact,
bushy variety doesn't need a lot of space, and it blooms
with very large clusters—a single cluster has up to 30
flowers! This variety is 'everblooming': it blooms non-
stop from summer through fall. Some of the other
Explorers bloom throughout summer, but are termed
'recurrent': they take brief breaks between periods of
peak flower production.

TIPS

* Although John Franklin blooms in large clusters,
  individual flowers are small, about 2 ½ inches
  (6 cm) across. They have fringed edges on their
  petals, similar to a carnation.

* If this rosebush is planted in an exposed area,
  expect some dead branch tips in spring. Don't
  worry about it; John Franklin recovers quickly
  and will bloom beautifully in summer.

* Released in 1980, this variety was named after Sir
  John Franklin, a British naval officer who charted
  much of the Canadian Arctic coastal region. Despite
  his accomplishments, he has become best known
  for the highly publicized, 12-year search for him
  and his lost ships in the mid-1800s. The search
  ended with the discovery that Franklin had died
  aboard his icebound ship in 1847 while attempting
  to be the first to sail the Northwest Passage.

Kakwa

There's something to be said for roses that only bloom once: they put everything they have into producing flowers all at once, resulting in one spectacular show. Kakwa bursts into bloom in late spring, at a time when other roses are just getting started. Beautiful, creamy white, double flowers, each about 2½ inches (6 cm) across, blanket the foliage and emit a powerful fragrance. The show lasts two to three weeks. Kakwa is a fine-textured, wide-spreading shrub, with dense, greyish-green foliage, chocolate-brown stems and tidy black rosehips.

Official Colour • white
Form • double
Scent • strong 'old rose' fragrance
ARS rating • (—)
Height • 3–4 feet (90–120 cm)
Spread • 3–4 feet (90–120 cm)
Blooms • late spring

TIPS

* Because it blooms only once each season, grow Kakwa with other plants that bloom at different times.

* The first roses of the season are irresistible. I often keep a few of Kakwa's flowers in small vases, to enjoy their incredible fragrance indoors.

* Kakwa is a tough, disease-resistant and adaptable rose that grows well in poor or sandy soil. It is somewhat drought tolerant.

* This variety is a *Rosa spinosissima* or Scots rose cultivar, which accounts for its unusual black rosehips. *Spinosissima* means 'the spiniest,' referring to the rose's very prickly branches. Kakwa was introduced in 1969 by John Wallace of Beaverlodge, Alberta.

Kakwa is one of the first roses to bloom in spring and is absolutely covered in very fragrant, creamy white flowers.

Louis Jolliet

Explorer Series Rose
climber

Official Colour •
medium pink
Form • double
Scent • light, spicy
ARS rating • (—)
Height •
4–5 feet (1.2–1.5 m)
Spread •
3–4 feet (90–120 cm)
Blooms • continuously
from early summer
to frost

Because it is one of the newest Explorers, Louis Jolliet may still be somewhat hard to find. Before a new variety becomes widely available, it takes a while to produce enough plants to match demand. And demand is sure to be high for this new climbing rose, with its extreme cold-hardiness, high disease resistance and masses of pink, 2 1/2-inch (7 cm), double flowers throughout the season. If I were a gambler, I'd wager that Louis Jolliet will soon become one of the world's most popular hardy climbing roses!

TIPS

• Unlike some hardy climbing roses, which take a few years to become established, even young plants of this variety bloom well.

• As an alternative to growing Louis Jolliet as a climber, allow it to spread and form a large, sprawling shrub.

• This variety has excellent resistance to both powdery mildew and blackspot.

• Louis Jolliet was introduced in 1990 and was named for the French-Canadian explorer who was co-discoverer of the Mississippi in 1673, and who later charted the Labrador Coast.

Louis Jolliet blooms abundantly, with more flowers than almost all other Explorer roses!

Mme. Hardy

Before you even see it, you know this rose is nearby—just follow your nose to find it. Mme. Hardy is one of the most fragrant roses, exuding a strong, sweet perfume with a hint of lemon. The very full flowers are about 3 to 3 1/2 inches (7.5–8.8 cm) across, and pure white with an interesting green button in the centre. Sometimes the petals show hints of blush-pink when they first open. Mme. Hardy has a long blooming period—the show lasts about a month!

Official Colour • white
Form • double
Scent • heavy
ARS rating • 9.2
Height •
   4–5 feet (1.2–1.5 m)
Spread •
   4–5 feet (1.2–1.5 m)
Blooms • summer

TIPS

* Cut these fragrant flowers for bouquets, or collect petals for potpourri. Mme. Hardy is a *Rosa damascena* (damask rose) hybrid, a type renowned for fragrance.

* You can plant this rose in partial shade, but it will have fewer flowers than if grown in full sun.

* Mme. Hardy is extremely resistant to blackspot. After 39 old garden roses were injected with this fungus in a 1992 test by Mississippi State University, Mme. Hardy showed no signs of the disease 16 days later.

* This variety can, however, be susceptible to powdery mildew. To help prevent mildew, water in the morning rather than at night, and don't crowd the plants; good air circulation helps to prevent this fungal disease.

* Every three or four years, prune this shrub down to a foot or two (30–60 cm) from the ground, and remove its oldest canes, as low as possible. To shape or shorten the shrub, prune just after flowering.

* This ancient variety dates back to 1832, and was named after the breeder's wife.

Mme. Hardy is one of the best and purest white roses. Each highly perfumed flower has more than 200 petals.

Marie Bugnet

Official Colour • white
Form • double
Scent • heavy
ARS rating • 8.2
Height •
  3–4 feet (90–120 cm)
Spread •
  3–4 feet (90–120 cm)
Blooms • repeatedly
  from early summer
  to frost

Marie Bugnet is one of the most compact shrub roses, with richly scented flowers all summer.

If you had a low hedge of Marie Bugnet lining a walkway, you'd want to find excuses to leave your house, if only to wander back and forth along the path, inhaling the roses' rich perfume. For years, I particularly enjoyed working in our vegetable garden, because the fragrance from a nearby bush of Marie Bugnet filled the air. This variety is one of the first roses to bloom in spring, and the show of snowy white, 3-inch (7.5 cm), double flowers continues in waves throughout summer and into fall.

TIPS

* Its small, compact size and long blooming period make Marie Bugnet perfect for growing in flowerbeds or as a low hedge. (See *Rose Hedges* on page 38.)

* Be persistent when shopping for this uncommon variety—it's hard to find. In fact, one catalogue actually listed it as 'extinct'! We know that this statement is false, because we buy these plants every year.

* Small, pale olive-green leaves against red stems provide a nice contrast to the snow-white flowers. Unlike many *Rosa rugosa* hybrids, Marie Bugnet does not form rosehips.

* This variety was introduced in 1963 by Georges Bugnet, who lived in Legal, Alberta, a town not far from my home. The name is French, pronounced 'boon-yay.'

Martin Frobisher

Martin Frobisher was the first rose in the Explorer series, introduced in 1968 at a time when choices in hardy roses were fairly limited. This variety offered a more dense, compact, pillar-shaped shrub, superior to many older hardy varieties. Best of all, it provided lots of fragrant, soft pink, 2-inch (5 cm), double flowers throughout summer! Almost three decades later, with 16 other roses added to the Explorer series, Martin Frobisher remains in high demand.

Official Colour • light pink
Form • double
Scent • sweet
ARS rating • 7.7
Height •
 5–6 feet (1.5–1.8 m)
Spread •
 4–5 feet (1.2–1.5 m)
Blooms • repeatedly from early summer to frost

TIPS

* Deadhead regularly to keep plants tidy, as the finished flowers tend to cling to the bush, particularly in wet weather.

* This variety is highly resistant to powdery mildew.

* In exposed areas, stems may die back to the snowline. Simply prune off the deadwood in spring. This vigorous shrub quickly regains its full height.

* This variety's namesake explorer, Sir Martin Frobisher, discovered what is now called Frobisher Bay (off Baffin Island), in 1576, while searching west of Greenland for a passage to Asia. For his heroism against the Spanish Armanda in 1588, he was knighted.

Martin Frobisher blooms with profuse waves of flowers all summer.

Max Graf

HARDY

128

Official Colour •
clear pink
Form • single
Scent • apple-like
ARS rating • 7.2
Height • 2–2 1/2 feet
(60–75 cm)
Spread • 8–10 feet
(2.4–3 m)
Blooms • early to
midsummer

I find it surprising that a rose as beautiful and useful as Max Graf is not more common in gardens. Few other roses make such a superb groundcover, nor can they match its combination of exceptional disease resistance, refreshing fragrance and extremely wide spread. At our greenhouses, these plants are among the most vigorous, forming thick, dense mats of glossy foliage. Max Graf blooms for over a month, and remains attractive even when not in flower.

TIPS

* Max Graf makes an outstanding groundcover.
  Its long, flexible canes root freely wherever they
  touch the ground, creating layers on top of layers,
  forming a dense, low bush with clusters of flowers.

* Although most often grown as a groundcover,
  this variety may also be trained as a climber.
  It looks stunning on an arbour or a trellis.

* For best results, grow Max Graf
  where it will have good snowcover
  throughout winter.

* This hardy variety dates back to
  1919. It is one of the most important
  roses in the breeding of today's best
  hardy rose varieties. Max Graf rarely
  produces rosehips, but about 50
  years ago, seed from a chance
  rosehip was used by William
  Kordes of Germany to create
  Rosa kordesii, the parent
  plant responsible for
  both the hardiness
  and the blackspot
  resistance found in
  Explorer roses.

*Max Graf has deep pink,
3–inch (7.5 cm) flowers. The
petals are satiny and crinkled
like a poppy.*

Morden Amorette

Parkland Series Rose

When gardeners ask for a compact rosebush for raised beds or borders, Morden Amorette is one of my first recommendations. This charming little rose brightens gardens all season, with an incredible show of 3-inch (7.5 cm), double flowers. It blooms continuously and profusely until frost, and has a good number of red rosehips in fall and winter. For a lovely display, grow perennial baby's breath behind Morden Amorette, imitating the classic look of a bouquet of roses.

Official Colour •
  deep pink
Form • double
Scent • light
ARS rating • (—)
Height • 1–2 feet
  (30–60 cm)
Spread • 1–2 feet
  (30–60 cm)
Blooms • continuously
  from early summer
  to frost

TIPS

❀ Because of its small size, this rose is ideal for growing in patio pots. For tips on winter protection for patio roses, see page 44.

❀ Deadhead to keep plants tidy and encourage continuous bloom.

❀ Morden Amorette has good resistance to powdery mildew and rust.

❀ 'Amorette' means 'little love'; Morden is the name of the town in Manitoba, Canada, where this rose was developed. It was introduced in 1977.

❋ *Morden Amorette is one of the smallest hardy roses, displaying a profusion of flowers all season.*

Morden Blush

Parkland Series Rose

Official Colour •
 light pink to ivory
Form • double
Scent • soft
ARS rating • (—)
Height •
 2–3 feet (60–90 cm)
Spread •
 2–3 feet (60–90 cm)
Blooms • continuously
 from early summer
 to frost

When one is simply not enough, you know the plant is outstanding. A gardener who bought her first Morden Blush last year loved it so much that she was back at our greenhouses first thing this spring to pick up half a dozen more. The colour of this rose is charming: the ivory flowers have blush-pink centres, which gradually fade to soft ivory. Morden Blush blooms profusely and continuously all season, with up to five, very full, double flowers per cluster.

TIPS

* Morden Blush is drought tolerant once it becomes established, but young plants need to be well-watered for the first growing season after planting. This variety also has great heat tolerance, but in hot sites, the flower colour is usually paler.

* These flowers are small, from 1 ½ to 2 inches (3.5–5 cm) across, but very full, with lots of petals. Use the attractive rosebuds for corsages or in wedding bouquets.

* This Canadian variety was introduced in 1988. It has good resistance to both powdery mildew and blackspot.

Morden Blush has the longest blooming period of any Prairie–developed shrub rose.

Morden Cardinette

If you want a brightly coloured, undemanding rose to grow in a patio pot, choose Morden Cardinette. With its dwarf, compact size and profuse clusters of bright, cardinal-red flowers throughout summer, it makes a lovely display, with perhaps some ivy and trailing lobelia tucked around the base. An added bonus is that Morden Cardinette has larger flowers than most varieties promoted as patio roses.

Official Colour •
  cardinal red
Form • double
Scent • light
ARS rating • (—)
Height • 2–2 ¹/₂ feet
  (60–75 cm)
Spread • 2–2 ¹/₂ feet
  (60–75 cm)
Blooms • continuously
  from early summer
  to frost

TIPS

* If you grow this rose in a patio pot, you will need to transplant it into your garden in fall, or protect as recommended on page 44. Unprotected roses will not survive winters in pots.

* This small shrub also looks splendid in raised beds or front flowerbeds.

* Usually, flowers are produced one to a stem or in small clusters of up to five, but occasionally you will find a huge cluster with as many as 15 flowers!

* This Canadian variety was introduced in 1980. It is highly resistant to rust.

Morden Cardinette is one of the smallest hardy rosebushes, with large, bright red, 3 ¹/₂-inch (8.5 cm) flowers produced throughout summer.

Morden Centennial

Parkland Series Rose

HARDY

Official Colour •
medium pink
Form • double
Scent • light, sweet
ARS rating • (—)
Height • 4–5 feet
(1.2–1.5 m)
Spread • 3–4 feet
(90–120 cm)
Blooms • repeatedly
from early summer
to frost

W hen Morden Centennial blooms at our greenhouses, very few customers can resist the urge to take home a pot or two. In gardens, it blooms so profusely that the flowers literally hide the foliage. This variety begins and ends the season with a bang; there are two main flushes of flowers, the first in early summer and the second in late summer to fall, with fewer flowers in between. The large, 4-inch (10 cm) flowers appear alone or in clusters of up to 15, followed by red rosehips that remain on branches throughout winter.

TIPS

* Although this rose is 'self-cleaning' (petals fall cleanly away from finished flowers), you'll have more blooms still if you deadhead. Snip off the entire cluster after blooming.

* Remember, however, to stop deadheading a few weeks before the end of summer. Allowing rosehips to form, signals rosebushes to prepare for winter.

* Morden Centennial has good resistance to powdery mildew and rust.

* For bushier plants with more side branches and flowers, be sure to prune back in spring before the leaves unfurl.

* This is a Canadian rose, developed at Agriculture Canada's research station in Morden, Manitoba, and introduced in honour of the town's centennial birthday in 1980.

Out of more than 250 rose varieties that we carry at our greenhouses, Morden Centennial is the top seller!

Morden Fireglow

Parkland Series Rose

Morden Fireglow looks more like a hybrid tea rose than a hardy shrub rose, with its shapely, 3-inch (7.5 cm) flowers, pointed rosebuds and glossy foliage. The brilliant colour of these flowers is very uncommon in a hardy rose, the result of careful selection during a long, complicated breeding program based on chemical analysis of flower pigment in parent plants. Petals are flaming scarlet on the undersides and orange-red on top, and the flowers are borne either one to a stem or in clusters of up to five.

Official Colour •
  bright scarlet
Form • double
Scent • light
ARS rating • (—)
Height • 3–3 ¹/₂ feet
  (90–105 cm)
Spread • 2–3 feet
  (60–90 cm)
Blooms • repeatedly
  from early summer
  to frost

TIPS

* This variety blooms on both old and new wood. The bush is 'self-cleaning,' which means petals fall cleanly from finished flowers.

* To encourage further blooming, deadhead regularly until a few weeks before the end of summer.

* These roses make lovely cutflowers. For the longest lasting bouquets, cut when flowerbuds are loose but still not open.

* Morden Fireglow is a Canadian rose that was introduced in 1989. It has good resistance to powdery mildew and rust.

The striking, fiery–red hue of Morden Fireglow is rare in hardy roses.

Morden Ruby

Parkland Series Rose

HARDY

Official Colour •
  ruby red
Form • double
Scent • light to none
ARS rating • (—)
Height • 3–4 feet
  (90–120 cm)
Spread • 3–3 ¹/₂ feet
  (90–105 cm)
Blooms • repeatedly
  from early summer
  to frost

The dark ruby–red hue of these striking flowers is unusual for a hardy rose.

O ne of the things I like best about Morden Ruby is its striking colour. Usually, these 2 ¹/₂- to 3 ¹/₂-inch (6–8.5 cm) flowers are pure, dark ruby-red, but occasionally, an odd, freckled flower with splashes of deeper red appears. Masses of long-lasting, large, very double flowers cover this small bush. It blooms most profusely in early and late summer, with fewer flowers in between.

TIPS

* This rosebush is the perfect size to fit into almost any flowerbed. I know one gardener who grows three in a row in the small flowerbed at the edge of her front porch, along with violet-blue speed-well and bright yellow pansies—a charming combination!

* In humid areas, Morden Ruby may be subject to blackspot. To reduce the chances of this fungal disease, water at the base of the plant and try not to wet the foliage.

* For bushier plants, prune hard in early spring before the leaves unfurl.

* Although this Canadian variety was intro-duced in 1977, it has still not been tested widely enough for an ARS rating to be assigned.

Nigel Hawthorne

'A rose is a rose is a rose is a rose' ... unless it's Nigel Hawthorne. This rose is so unusual-looking that there is some doubt as to whether it is truly a rose. Some botanists don't believe it belongs in the *Rosa* group at all, and classify this and Euphrates (see page 105) as *Hulthemia persica*. Regardless of its botanical name, Nigel Hawthorne is sure to be a knockout in your garden. The distinctive, 2- to 2 1/2-inch (5–6 cm), scarlet-eyed flowers are bright rosy-salmon when they open, and gradually fade to a soft salmon, resulting in flowers of different shades in a single cluster.

Official Colour •
   rosy-salmon with
   deep scarlet eye
Form • single
Scent • light, spicy
ARS rating • (—)
Height • 2 1/2–3 feet
   (75–90 cm)
Spread • 3–4 feet
   (90–120 cm)
Blooms • repeatedly
   from early summer
   to frost

TIPS

* Nigel Hawthorne blooms profusely in early summer, with fewer flowers thereafter.

* This rare rose is difficult to find, because it is harder to propagate than many others, and is in high demand.

* Unlike its partner Euphrates, Nigel Hawthorne is not shade tolerant.

* I grow Nigel Hawthorne in an exposed area next to a walkway, beside the back deck. It has survived unscathed, with little to no winter dieback at all, likely because of a deep snowcover that increases each time we shovel the walk and deck.

* This variety was introduced in 1989, and is named after the British actor Nigel Hawthorne, who is said to be particularly fond of shrub roses.

At our greenhouses, Nigel Hawthorne always sells out before it even hits the sales floor.

Nozomi

Hardy Shrub Rose

HARDY

136

Official Colour •
pearl pink
Form • single
Scent • light
ARS rating • 7.9
Height • 1¹/₂–2 feet
(45–60 cm)
Spread • 5–6 feet
(1.5–1.8 m)
Blooms • summer

Nozomi grows as a beautiful groundcover, scrambling over nearby bushes, and producing a charming display all season. For two to three weeks in summer, a multitude of beautiful, starry, 1-inch (2.5 cm) flowers in small clusters cover its arching, plum-coloured branches. For a different effect, try growing Nozomi as a miniature climber—its dark, shiny leaves and trailing branches look wonderful against a trellis even when the plant is not in bloom.

TIPS

* Have patience if you are growing Nozomi as a groundcover. It takes a year or two after planting before the plants fill in and branches and foliage become dense.

* Nozomi is shade tolerant and grows well in poor soil.

* This rose can be susceptible to blackspot. To reduce chances of this fungal disease, avoid wetting the foliage. Water at the base of the plant rather than from overhead.

* This variety was introduced in 1968 from Japan; its name means 'hope' in Japanese. The small leaves and flowers are evidence of the miniature rose in its parentage.

Nozomi is a wonderful groundcover rose, with long, trailing branches and masses of starry flowers.

Pavement Roses

Hardy Shrub Roses

I have always thought that the name 'Pavement' was a rather unfortunate choice for such a lovely series of roses. Recently, however, I discovered that this is owing to the difference in word usage between Europeans and North Americans: what they call pavement, we call sidewalk. Now I think of these roses as 'sidewalk roses,' perfectly suited for boulevards or along sidewalks, because they bloom profusely all summer regardless of heat, drought or poor soil. There are seven varieties of Pavement Roses to choose from—all have fragrant flowers.

Official Colour •
  pink, red, white
Form • semi-double to
  double
Scent • fragrant
ARS rating • (—)
Height • 2–2 1/2 feet
  (60–75 cm)
Spread • 3–4 feet
  (90–120 cm)
Blooms • repeatedly
  from early summer to
  frost

Dwarf Pavement is a very compact rose with bright pink, semi-double flowers. **Showy Pavement** has arching branches and pink, semi-double flowers. **Pierrette Pavement** looks similar, but has darker pink flowers and an exceptionally strong, award-winning fragrance. **Purple Pavement** is very showy, with clusters of purplish-red, semi-double flowers with yellow hearts and dark red rosehips in fall. **Scarlet Pavement** produces dark red rosehips alongside its fuchsia-red, semi-double flowers. **Snow Pavement** is blush-white with double flowers. **Foxi Pavement** has deep purple-pink, single flowers and a strong 'rose' fragrance.

Showy Pavement

TIPS

* Pavement Roses are rugosa hybrids, renowned for their rugged hardiness and ability to tolerate not only extreme cold, but also heat, drought, and intense sunlight or partial shade.

* This series may also be the most salt tolerant of any roses yet developed. All of the Pavement Roses are superb for coastal gardens or planting alongside driveways or roads on which salt is used in winter.

Pavement Roses are among the lowest–maintenance roses, as tough as they are beautiful, with lovely, 3–inch (7.5 cm) flowers all summer.

* Deadhead regularly until a few weeks before the end of summer to encourage further blooming.

* Pavement Series Roses were introduced in 1986, from Germany. They all have excellent resistance to blackspot and powdery mildew.

Scarlet Pavement

Snow Pavement

Quadra

R ed remains the most popular colour for roses, and those gardeners who want red roses are often quite adamant about the shade: not scarlet, not vermilion, but a true, rich, deep, dark red. This is the colour of Quadra, one of the newest roses in the Explorer series. Its velvety flowers are larger with far more petals than many of the others, similar to an old-fashioned rose. Quadra blooms repeatedly throughout the season, most abundantly in early summer, with stunning flowers from 3 to 4 inches (7.5–10 cm) across, alone or in clusters of up to four.

Explorer Series Rose climber

Official Colour •
  dark red
Form • double
Scent • little to none
ARS rating • (—)
Height •
  5–6 feet (1.5–1.8 m)
Spread •
  4–5 feet (1.2–1.5 m)
Blooms • repeatedly
  from early summer
  to frost

TIPS

* Plant Quadra in flowerbeds as a backdrop to brightly coloured annuals or silvery perennials, such as sage and snow-in-summer.

* This rose makes a great feature shrub, surrounded by low blue junipers to offset its dark red flowers.

* Versatile Quadra can also be trained to climb on a trellis.

* This variety is resistant to powdery mildew and blackspot.

* Introduced in 1994, this variety was named after the 18th-century Spanish naval officer Juan Francisco de la Bodega y Quadra, whose voyages ranged from Mexico to Alaska. In 1792 he battled the British in the waters off Vancouver Island.

Quadra blooms with magnificent, rich red flowers all season!

Red Frau Dagmar Hartopp

Official Colour •
   deep magenta
Form • single
Scent • light
ARS rating • (—)
Height •
   3 feet (90 cm)
Spread •
   4–5 feet (1.2–1.5 m)
Blooms • repeatedly
   from early summer
   to frost

When Red Frau Dagmar Hartopp blooms, everyone stops to look at its flowers.

In the late 1980s, in a European garden of Frau Dagmar Hartopp roses, a lone rosebush stood out amongst the profusion of plants with pale pink flowers. Unlike the others, its petals were a striking deep magenta. That rosebush was carefully cultivated to produce a new variety: Red Frau Dagmar Hartopp. It is a very showy rose, with all the best features of the original Frau Dagmar Hartopp but in a dazzling, new colour.

TIPS

* This rose makes a wonderful hedge, because its thorny branches create a formidable barrier.

* Red Frau Dagmar Hartopp blooms until stopped by fall frosts, with cupped 3- to 3 1/2-inch (7.5–8.5 cm) flowers. It produces abundant cherry tomato–like roseships, and is one of the best roses for fall colour.

* Most roses need full sun—eight or more hours of sunlight every day—but Red Frau Dagmar Hartopp does well even with shade for half the day.

* Like all *Rosa rugosa* cultivars, Red Frau Dagmar Hartopp is very vigorous and highly resistant to blackspot and powdery mildew.

Red Rugosa

Rugosa roses (*Rosa rugosa*) are noted for their hardiness, longevity and strongly scented flowers. They are so hardy that they need no winter protection except in the coldest areas (-50° F / -45° C) and so tough that they can be grown along seashores or roadsides, withstanding winter salt spray from passing cars. Best of all, they bloom all summer, from June to September, with lots of large, single flowers that emit a strong, sweet-clove perfume. The Red Rugosa doesn't live up to its name—the flowers are a striking magenta-purple rather than true red.

Official Colour •
   brilliant magenta
Form • single
Scent • fragrant
ARS rating • 8.2
Height •
   5–6 feet (1.5–1.8 m)
Spread •
   5–6 feet (1.5–1.8 m)
Blooms • repeatedly
   from early summer
   to frost

TIPS

* The name *rugosa* means 'wrinkled' and refers to the texture of the dark green leaves, which are distinctively crinkled, as if they had been folded up accordion-style.

* Rugosa roses thrive even in dry conditions and poor soil. They are highly resistant to blackspot and powdery mildew, the two most common rose diseases.

* With its large, gleaming red-orange rosehips and brilliant orange fall foliage, this variety is one of the showiest roses at the end of the growing season.

* The Red Rugosa (*Rosa rugosa rubra*) dates back to at least the 18th century.

This variety has the largest blooms of all single-flowered rugosa roses, each one from 4 to 5 inches (10–12.5 cm) across.

Red-leaf Rose

Species Rose

HARDY
142

Official Colour • pink
Form • single
Scent • light
ARS rating • 8.4
Height •
  5–6 feet (1.5–1.8 m)
Spread •
  5–6 feet (1.5–1.8 m)
Blooms • late spring

The Red-leaf Rose provides four seasons of beauty, and is one of the few roses that is favoured more for its foliage than its flowers. It blooms rather sparsely in late spring, with clusters of lightly scented, starry, mauve-pink flowers, but the colourful foliage is stunning throughout summer. In fall, the reddish-violet leaves and big, oval rosehips contrast nicely with the usual autumn oranges and yellows, and in winter, the purple-red stems make a strong statement against a snowy backdrop.

TIPS

* Although the Red-leaf Rose is said to be shade tolerant, we have found it is more impressive grown in full sun. In shady sites, the foliage colour is less intense, and blackspot can be a problem.

* The Red-leaf Rose makes a magnificent hedge.

* Offset the foliage colour by planting yellow or white flowers nearby.

* Snip branches of foliage to add dramatic flare to your floral arrangements. Young, purple shoots are particularly attractive, and the nearly thornless stems are easy to handle. Don't remove too much foliage at one time, to avoid damaging your plant.

The botanical name Rosa glauca *refers to the dramatic blue cast of the foliage. Formerly, this rose was known as* Rosa rubrifolia, *which simply means 'red–leaf rose.' But in addition to the leaves, almost everything about this unusual rose is red: the brownish–red calyxes that encase the flowers, the dark reddish–violet stems and the bright red–purple rosehips.*

Reine des Violettes

Old Garden Rose

R eine des Violettes is a stunning rose. The clusters of deep velvety purple-red flowers soften to shades of mauve-grey and violet as their cupped shape flattens out. These very double, 3-inch (7.5 cm) flowers have a delicious, heady fragrance. Reine des Violettes blooms most profusely in early summer. The grey-green foliage has a faint peppery scent. Because of its nearly thornless stems, researchers are attempting to isolate the 'thornless' gene from this variety.

Official Colour • mauve
Form • very double
Scent • heavy
ARS rating • 8.0
Height •
  3 feet (90 cm)
Spread •
  3 feet (90 cm)
Blooms • repeatedly
  from early summer
  to frost

HARDY

143

TIPS

* For the best flowers and most profuse bloom, plant the rosebush in a very sunny site with rich, well-drained soil and good air circulation.

* To encourage further flowering, deadhead regularly until a few weeks before the end of summer. Late-season flowers tend to have richer colour.

* This rose is what we call a 'heavy feeder.' Be sure to fertilize regularly as recommended on page 49.

* This rose can be susceptible to blackspot. To help prevent this fungal disease, avoid wetting the foliage. Water at the base of the plant rather than from overhead.

* This variety was introduced in 1860 and is also known as Queen of the Violets. It is a hybrid perpetual rose, a type that was among the most popular roses in the 1800s.

Although there are no true blue roses, Reine des Violettes is among those roses that are closest to this colour.

Rosa Mundi

Old Garden Rose

HARDY

144

Official Colour •
pink blend
Form • semi-double
Scent • fragrant
ARS rating • 8.6
Height •
2–3 feet (60–90 cm)
Spread •
2–3 feet (60–90 cm)
Blooms • midsummer

No two of Rosa Mundi's beautiful, striped flowers are exactly alike.

Rosa Mundi is a rose that once seen is never forgotten. These distinctive, flat flowers are blush-white, each with a unique pattern of rich rose-pink and red stripes around golden-yellow stamens. Each flower is 3 to 3 ¹/₂ inches (7.5–8.5 cm) across. Rosa Mundi blooms only once, but is a show-stopper while its stems are weighed down with flowers. It forms a nice, compact bush with matte apple-green foliage and bright red rosehips in fall. Rosa Mundi is the oldest striped rose variety.

TIPS

* Like many old garden roses, Rosa Mundi is shade tolerant and grows well even with only afternoon sun.

* Don't over-fertilize this rose because the flowers will have less pronounced stripes.

* This variety is extremely resistant to blackspot. Thirty-nine old garden roses were injected with this fungus in a 1992 test by Mississippi State University, and 16 days later Rosa Mundi showed no signs of the disease.

* Rosa Mundi is a 'sport' or seedling of *Rosa gallica officinalis*, the Apothecary's Rose. These roses are among the best for making potpourri, as they have the unusual ability to retain fragrance when their petals are dried and powdered.

* This ancient variety is said to have been named after Fair Rosamund, mistress of Henry II, which would date it back to the 12th century. It is often listed by its botanical name, *Rosa gallica versicolor*.

Scabrosa

S cabrosa is a stunning rose, with immense, rich purple-red flowers about 5 inches (12.5 cm) across, offset by sulphur yellow stamens. The show continues all season, with abundant clusters, each with five or more flowers, and a delicious, cinnamon-sweet fragrance that reminds me of carnations. This rose is one of the most attractive roses in fall, with its orange foliage and large rosehips like cherry tomatoes.

Official Colour •
   mauve-pink
Form • single
Scent • strong, sweet
ARS rating • 7.5
Height •
   5–6 feet (1.5–1.8 m)
Spread •
   4–5 feet (1.2–1.5 m)
Blooms • repeatedly
   from early summer
   to frost

TIPS

* This large, dense bush makes a great background to other flowers. It is shade tolerant, performing well with sun for only half the day.

* With its large size, long blooming period and showy fall colour, Scabrosa makes a wonderful hedge. See *Rose Hedges* on page 38.

* Scabrosa is a *Rosa rugosa* hybrid, introduced in 1950. It re-blooms better than most rugosas, and has distinctive, wrinkled, somewhat glossy foliage that is rarely troubled by disease.

* This variety is one of the hardiest of all roses.

Scabrosa is one of the largest–flowered hardy roses.

Schneezwerg

Official Colour •
    snow-white
Form • semi-double
Scent • strong, sweet
ARS rating • 7.5
Height •
    3–4 feet (90–120 cm)
Spread •
    3–4 feet (90–120 cm)
Blooms • continuously
    from early summer
    to frost

Pure snow–white flowers against rich, dark foliage make Schneezwerg a dazzling rose.

Our nursery manager, Shane Neufeld, loves this rose because it is 'such a rugosa.' By this phrase, he means that this hybrid has all the best characteristics of its parent *Rosa rugosa:* disease-free, glossy foliage that turns bright orange and yellow in fall; sweetly scented flowers all summer; extreme cold-hardiness; and the ability to thrive for years and years under almost any conditions. Schneezwerg's bright white, 3-inch (7.5 cm) flowers have pale yellow stamens, and are borne in clusters of 3 to 10.

TIPS

* Like its parent rugosa, this versatile variety is tolerant of shade and poor soil, and makes a superb hedge. Schneezwerg looks different than most rugosas, however, with twiggy growth forming a more compact bush.

* This variety is one of the showiest roses in fall, with colourful leaves and abundant orange-red hips, often produced while the plant is still flowering.

* You may find Schneezwerg listed as Snowdwarf, which is the translation of its name. The variety was introduced in 1912.

Simon Fraser

Official Colour •
  medium pink
Form • semi-double
Scent • light
ARS rating • (—)
Height • 2–2 1/2 feet
  (60–75 cm)
Spread • 2–3 feet
  (60–90 cm)
Blooms • continuously
  from early summer
  to frost

One of the newest roses in the Explorer series is Simon Fraser. We were able to obtain only a few when these roses were first released, and within days, every single one was sold. Even when young, Simon Fraser blooms so profusely that the 2-inch (5 cm) flowers literally hide the foliage. Most hardy roses take breaks between periods of bloom, but this variety blooms non-stop from early summer to frost. Simon Fraser is a stunning shrub; it is the perfect size to grow in flowerbeds or borders, and it acts as a very decorative showpiece throughout the season.

TIPS

* Young plants have lots of flowers, but the first roses of the season are usually single, with semi-double or double flowers produced as summer progresses. Once plants get older, their flower form is more consistently semi-double.

* Simon Fraser's leaves are dark green and semi-glossy, and the branches have only a few prickles.

* This variety has good resistance to powdery mildew and blackspot.

* Introduced in 1992, this variety is named for the explorer Simon Fraser, who in the years 1805–8 founded the earliest settlements in central British Columbia and after whom the Fraser River is named.

 *Simon Fraser blooms longer than almost every other hardy rose!*

Stanwell Perpetual

Official Colour • white
Form • double
Scent • strong, sweet
ARS rating • 8.6
Height •
3–5 feet (90–150 cm)
Spread •
3–5 feet (90–150 cm)
Blooms • continuously
from late spring
to frost

Stanwell Perpetual has large, fragrant, double flowers that open a soft blue-pink in colour and gently fade to white. The flowers are very full, from 3 to 3 1/2 inches (7.5–8.5 cm) across, and borne one to a stem. I often cut them for bouquets or rosebowls; curiously, their sweet fragrance seems stronger indoors than in the garden. Stanwell Perpetual is a dense, twiggy bush with long, arching, prickly shoots and grey-green, highly disease-resistant foliage. This variety blooms non-stop all season, with bigger, darker flowers in fall.

TIPS

* With its dense foliage and compact form, Stanwell Perpetual makes a great hedge.

* Don't worry if the blue-green foliage has a curiously mottled purple look—this is not a disease but merely the leaves' natural appearance.

* Stanwell Perpetual is one of the longest-blooming roses, starting its show with a burst of flowers in spring and continuing to bloom even after several hard frosts in fall.

* This English variety was introduced in 1838. It is a *Rosa spinosissima* cultivar, which accounts for its prickly branches.

Superb Tuscan

To me, part of the charm of old garden roses is their age—I find pleasure in simply gazing at the flowers and knowing that the same variety has graced gardens for centuries. Gallica roses are the earliest recorded roses cultivated in Europe, and Superb Tuscan, a variety that has been grown for over 150 years, is among the nicest of the gallica roses. Its highly fragrant, cupped flowers are 3 1/2 to 4 inches (8.5–10 cm) across, in a lovely shade of deep velvety maroon fading to purple.

Official Colour • mauve
Form • double
Scent • strong, sweet
ARS rating • 8.2
Height • 3–3 1/2 feet
 (90–105 cm)
Spread • 2 1/2–3 feet
 (75–90 cm)
Blooms • midsummer

TIPS

* Plant Superb Tuscan near a walkway or garden bench, where you will be able to enjoy its rich fragrance. It does best in an open site.

* Old garden roses generally are not fussy. Superb Tuscan grows well even in poor soils, forming a neat, upright bush with plentiful, dark green foliage.

* Prune away old, unproductive canes after the bush finishes flowering.

* This variety dates back to 1837 or earlier. It is otherwise known as Double Velvet, Double Tuscany, Superb Tuscany, Tuscany Superb and Tuscany Supreme.

Superb Tuscan has a rich, sweet fragrance and deep, velvety flowers—as close to black as you can get in a rose.

Sweetbriar Rose

Official Colour • pink
Form • single
Scent • 'true rose'
 fragrance
ARS rating • 8.6
Height •
 8–10 feet (2.4–3 m)
Spread •
 5–6 feet (1.5–1.8 m)
Blooms • late spring

The fragrance of most roses comes from the flowers, but the wonderful, sweet-apple scent of the Sweetbriar Rose comes from its leaves. This lovely fragrance is strongest just after a rainfall, often scenting the entire garden. Sweetbriar Rose is an impressive arching shrub that grows to about 10 feet (3 m) tall. It blooms in mid-June, with lots of small, blush-pink, 2-inch (5 cm), single flowers, which are also scented with a 'true rose' fragrance.

TIPS

* Be sure to plant this rose well away from walkways. 'Briar' means 'thorny bush,' and the many hooked thorns that line the Sweetbriar's thick branches can easily tear skin. This rose makes a superb, though wicked, hedge, with abundant, bright orange, oval rosehips that last well into winter.

* Sweetbriar Roses are ideal for growing under a window. You'll not only be able to enjoy their fragrance from both indoors and outdoors, but also to gain a dense, thorny barrier against intruders.

* The Sweetbriar Rose (*Rosa eglanteria*) is highly disease resistant. It was cultivated prior to 1551, and is sometimes called eglantine. During the 19th century, it was the preferred rootstock for grafting rose standards.

✳ *The most prominent feature of the Sweetbriar Rose is the sweet–apple fragrance of its foliage. Lightly rub a leaf between your fingers to release the fresh scent.*

✳ *'... a bank whereon the wild thyme blows, where oxlips and the nodding violet grows, Quite overcanopied with luscious woodbine, with sweet musk roses, and with eglantine.'*
—William Shakespeare,
A Midsummer Night's Dream

The Hunter

Hardy Shrub

I n the opinion of some gardeners, The Hunter has no equal. A customer came to the greenhouses one summer, looking for this variety. Unfortunately, we were sold out so suggested another variety, but for this man, nothing else would do. He ordered 50 plants of The Hunter and came out next spring to collect them. Now, somewhere north of my town, a long row of bushy shrubs, with fragrant, rich red, double flowers, outlines his acreage. He finally has his dream hedge of The Hunter flowers.

Official Colour •
  bright crimson
Form • double
Scent • fragrant
ARS rating: (—)
Height • 4–4 1/2 feet
  (1.2–1.4 m)
Spread • 3–3 1/2 feet
  (90–105 cm)
Blooms • repeatedly
  from early summer
  to frost

TIPS

* The Hunter is a tidy rosebush with shiny, dark green leaves. It makes an impressive hedge. Even if part of the hedge is shaded, this variety grows well.

* Although this rose tolerates poor soil, it does best in a moist, well-drained site.

* The Hunter blooms in waves throughout summer, with flowers about 2 1/2 to 3 inches (6–7.5 cm) across.

* This variety is a *Rosa rugosa* hybrid from England, introduced in 1961.

The rich crimson colour of these fragrant roses makes The Hunter a popular variety.

Hardy Shrub Rose climber

Official Colour • white
Form • semi-double
Scent • little to none
ARS rating • (—)
Height •
  15–18 feet (4.6–5.5 m)
Spread •
  5–6 feet (1.5–1.8 m)
Blooms • summer

The Polar Star is the largest, most vigorous and hardiest climbing rose.

The Polar Star

In the show garden at our greenhouses, The Polar Star grows on a trellis, putting on a spectacular show for about three weeks in midsummer. Clusters of small, pure white, double flowers, each about 1 to 1 1/2 inches (2.5–3.5 cm) across, cover its branches, enticing customers from across the parking lot to head over for a closer look. To keep The Polar Star confined to its trellis, we cut off a few outside canes each spring. This variety is a rampant rose that would easily climb as high as a second-storey window.

TIPS

❋ When shopping for this rose, make sure you get the right one. There is a hybrid tea rose named Polar Star—*The* Polar Star is the hardy climber. To add to the confusion, The Polar Star is also known as Polstjärnan, Polestar, White Star of Finland, White Rose of Finland, The Wasa Star and Wasastiernan!

❋ Left unchecked, The Polar Star makes a superb groundcover, spreading up to 18 feet (5.5 m) wide and 8 to 10 feet (2.4–3 m) tall, rooting wherever it touches the ground. Choose a hillside or a site through which you do not plan to walk ever again, for these very thorny canes create a formidable barrier.

❋ Because this disease-resistant rose blooms on old wood, do not prune heavily or remove a lot of canes in spring. If you do so, you will have few flowers that summer.

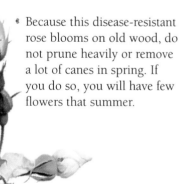

Thérèse Bugnet

Hardy Shrub Rose

It's not often that one discovers a rose with close ties to home. For me, that is one of the endearing qualities of Thérèse Bugnet, a distinctively beautiful rose with lovely, pink, ruffled flowers. This variety was developed over a 25-year period by Georges Bugnet, a man who won awards for his work in hybridizing roses. Mr. Bugnet lived in Legal, Alberta, a small town not far from where I live, and in 1981, died in St. Albert, Alberta, my hometown. Unfortunately, I never had the chance to meet him.

Official Colour •
  medium pink
Form • double
Scent • fragrant
ARS rating • 8.2
Height •
  5–6 feet (1.5–1.8 m)
Spread •
  4–5 feet (1.2–1.5 m)
Blooms • repeatedly
  from early summer
  to frost

TIPS

❀ Thérèse Bugnet has dark red rosebuds that open to frilly, mauve-pink flowers, about 3 to 4 inches (7.5–10 cm) across. Expect a great show of flowers in early summer, with brief breaks between abundant waves of blooms afterward.

❀ To encourage further blooming, deadhead regularly until a few weeks before the end of summer.

❀ This rose blooms on old wood. It is a naturally shapely bush that rarely needs pruning, but if you must, prune after the first flush of flowers finishes in early summer. Don't remove a lot of canes or prune in spring, because by doing so, you are snipping off your future flowers.

❀ The attractive grey-green leaves turn orange and scarlet in fall, with abundant orange rosehips that provide food for birds. Colourful red canes provide a fine display through winter.

❀ This versatile variety is tolerant of heat, wind, alkaline soil and late frosts. It was introduced in 1950, and named for Mr. Bugnet's daughter.

❁ *Thérèse Bugnet has been called one of the cold-hardiest roses in the world, still blooming to the tips after –35° F (–37° C) winters.*

Hardy Shrub Rose

Topaz Jewel

Official Colour •
medium yellow
fading to cream
Form • double
Scent • fruity
ARS rating • 7.4
Height • 3–3 1/2 feet
(90–105 cm)
Spread • 3–3 1/2 feet
(90–105 cm)
Blooms • repeatedly
from early summer
to frost

Topaz Jewel will always be one of my most-loved roses. I find its clusters of sweetly scented, butter-cream-yellow flowers irresistible. Because of its compact, bushy form and beautiful flower colour—yellow roses are always in high demand—this variety sells like hot-cakes at our greenhouses. Flower colour deepens in cool weather, and softens to cream in hot sun. The flowers become paler as they age, providing a nice array of yellow hues against dark green foliage.

TIPS

* Topaz Jewel blooms in waves throughout the season, starting with a big splash in early summer. Its 3- to 3 1/2-inch (7.5–8.5 cm) flowers are produced in clusters of five to eight, and sometimes more.

* Finished flowers fall cleanly from this bush, so deadheading is not required to keep plants tidy. To encourage more blooming, however, it helps to remove the entire cluster after petals drop.

* Although this is a *Rosa rugosa* hybrid, it is less hardy than other varieties. For best results, plant it in a site where it is easy to cover with snow. Keep the entire shrub almost completely covered throughout winter.

* This disease-resistant variety was introduced in 1987.

Topaz Jewel is an uncommon variety and to the best of my knowledge, the only yellow rugosa rose.

White Rugosa

Species Rose

White Rugosa is like Red Rugosa in most respects, except for the difference in flower colour, and that the White Rugosa is a denser bush. Long, pointed, blush-pink rosebuds open to large, pure snow-white flowers, which are up to 4 inches (10 cm) across. This rose makes a superb hedge. It is one of the few species roses that blooms all summer, and one of the best roses for fall colour. The foliage turns brilliant orange, and it is offset by large, gleaming orange-red rosehips that remain on the bush's branches through winter. White Rugosa is considered by many rose experts to be one of the most fragrant roses.

Official Colour •
pure white
Form • single
Scent • heavy
ARS rating • 9.0
Height • 6 feet (1.8 m)
Spread • 6 feet (1.8 m)
Blooms • repeatedly
from early summer
to frost

TIPS

❁ Rugosa roses are renowned for their ability to tolerate not only extreme cold, but also heat, drought and intense sunlight or partial shade.

❁ Another wonderful feature of rugosa roses is their outstanding resistance to blackspot and their tolerance of salty soils, which makes them particularly good for growing near roadways or driveways, where de-icing salt is used in winter.

❁ This species is native to China and Japan. The White Rugosa (*Rosa rugosa* 'Alba') has been cultivated since about 1870. 'Alba' is Latin for 'white.'

White Rugosa blooms all summer, with large, extremely fragrant, poppy–like flowers.

Explorer Series Rose climber

Official Colour •
    deep pink
Form • semi-double
Scent • light
ARS rating • 9.4
Height •
    8–10 feet (2.4–3 m)
Spread •
    5–6 feet (1.5–1.8 m)
Blooms • repeatedly
    from early summer
    to frost

William Baffin

The strong, arching branches of this vigorous and robust climber are dramatically blanketed in masses of flowers all summer long. William Baffin grows quickly, towering above a doorway or arch in just three to four years, with a splendid profusion of 2 ¹/₂- to 3-inch (6–7.5 cm) flowers. This variety becomes very full, branching well with stiff stems and lots of leaves behind immense flower clusters. A single cluster has up to 30 flowers!

TIPS

* William Baffin can be grown as an impressive climber against a trellis. If allowed to sprawl unchecked, it forms a large bush.

* This variety is a rose that needs no fussing at all. It is highly resistant to blackspot and powdery mildew, requires very little pruning and can be left unprotected on the trellis throughout winter.

* This Canadian variety was introduced in 1983. It is named after the explorer who in 1616 discovered Lancaster Sound, but did not realize it was the entrance to the Northwest Passage. On the same voyage, Baffin and Captain Robert Bylot sailed farther north than any other explorer for the next 236 years.

William Baffin is one of the largest and hardiest climbing roses.

Wingthorn Rose

Species Rose

T he outstanding feature of the Wingthorn Rose is its beautiful red thorns, which gleam like rubies in the sunlight. Quite often, several tall, thorny stems rise above this bushy shrub, like long flowerspikes, causing passersby to do a double take and stare in amazement. It is for these thorny spikes rather than the flowers that most gardeners choose the Wingthorn Rose, although some grow it as a barrier to keep unwanted visitors, such as cats or dogs, out of the yard. As shrubs mature, the huge hooked thorns grow larger, each one eventually becoming the size of your thumb!

Official Colour • white
Form • single
Scent • light
ARS rating • 8.4
Height •
  6–8 feet (1.8–2.4 m)
Spread •
  5–6 feet (1.5–1.8 m)
Blooms • late spring to
  early summer

HARDY
157

TIPS

❋ For the best effect, plant three Wingthorns together, spaced about 3 feet (90 cm) apart. This variety grows well in sun or shade.

❋ Bright white, 1 ¹/₂-inch (3.5 cm) flowers with pronounced yellow centres bloom in late spring to early summer, followed by orange-red, oval rosehips.

❋ Expect a fair bit of dieback over winter—as much as half its height, or even to the snowline. This dieback is not a concern, because this shrub should be pruned back hard anyhow, since the showiest, reddest thorns are on the new growth.

❋ You may find this rose listed under other names, such as *Rosa sericea pteracantha*, Red Thorn Rose or Blood Thorn Rose. It has been cultivated since 1890 and originates from the Himalayas.

✻ *A curiosity among roses, the Wingthorn Rose is grown for its translucent red thorns rather than its flowers.*

Winnipeg Parks

HARDY

158

Official Colour •
  dark pink-red
Form • double
Scent • light
ARS rating • 7.5
Height •
  1–2 feet (30–60 cm)
Spread •
  1–2 feet (30–60 cm)
Blooms • continuously
  from early summer
  to frost

I once had a customer who couldn't decide between a red or a pink rose. 'Get one of each,' I suggested, but she said she only had room for a single plant. 'Well then,' I told her, 'the rose you want is Winnipeg Parks.' Its 3 1/2-inch (8.5 cm), double flowers are red when they first open and then fade to dark pink-red, with dark pink on the undersides of the petals. The bush is small enough to easily fit into almost any garden, and it blooms profusely all summer. For this woman, and many other gardeners, Winnipeg Parks is the perfect rose.

TIPS

* Winnipeg Parks blooms continuously for almost three months, beginning with an impressive display in early summer.

* This vigorous, tight, compact shrub makes a wonderful addition to flowerbeds or shrub borders.

* In cool weather and in fall, the foliage develops an attractive reddish tinge.

* This variety has good resistance to powdery mildew and rust.

* Introduced in 1993, this Canadian variety was named for the centennial anniversary of the City of Winnipeg's Parks and Recreation Department.

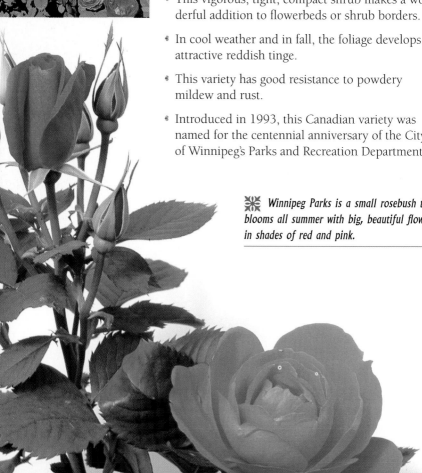

Winnipeg Parks is a small rosebush that blooms all summer with big, beautiful flowers in shades of red and pink.

FAVOURITE TENDER ROSES

'All the world glows with roses, roses, roses.'
—Saul Chernihovsky (1875–1943),
Russian-born American poet

Tender roses have beautiful flowers, similar to the roses you might find at florists, in a wide range of colours. These flowers make wonderful bouquets, and the rosebushes bloom over a long period—most of them all summer. Tender roses include some of the best-known types—hybrid teas, grandifloras, floribundas and miniature roses—all of which are often grown for exhibition. English roses are relative newcomers within the world of roses.

All tender roses require winter protection. See *What to Do in Fall, Winter & Spring* on page 61 for details.

English Roses

English roses are a relatively new class of roses, and are particularly noted for their full, very double flowers and outstanding fragrance. These roses are the result of years of breeding in England by David Austin, who combined the fragrance and delicate pastel hues of old garden roses with the sturdiness and re-blooming ability of modern roses.

Austin crossed modern climbers, floribundas and hybrid teas with two of the oldest rose families known: the gallicas and the damasks. His line of hybrid roses was so distinct from other roses that it qualified as a whole new race. English roses have become widely grown in North America over the last decade; we planted our first English rose over six years ago.

Tender roses bloom in a rainbow of colours, including pastel shades and unusual bicolours.

Favourite English Roses

Abraham Darby	Heritage
Charles Austin	L.D. Braithwaite
Charles Rennie Mackintosh	Lilian Austin
English Garden	Mary Rose
Evelyn	Peach Blossom
Fair Bianca	Redouté
Fisherman's Friend	St. Swithun
Gertrude Jekyll	The Alexandra Rose
Glamis Castle	The Countryman
Graham Thomas	The Pilgrim

❋ *Worldwide, about 3 million English roses will be grown for sale this year.*

Abraham Darby

Floribunda Roses

'Floribunda' means 'abundance of flowers.' These roses bloom with clusters of flowers from early summer to the first killing frost in fall. Expect one big flush of flowers in early summer, another a few weeks later, and fewer flowers in between and after. Floribunda roses are generally shorter than hybrid tea roses. They are considered hardier, but still need protection to survive winter. (The variety Sally Holmes is actually a tender shrub rose, but it can be treated like a floribunda.)

Floribunda roses, such as Europeana (above), produce many flowers on a single stem, resulting in an impressive display of colour.

Favourite Floribunda Roses

Apricot Nectar	Livin' Easy
Escapade	Nearly Wild
Europeana	Regensberg
Eyepaint	Sally Holmes
First Edition	Sexy Rexy
Gene Boerner	Showbiz
Gruss an Aachen	Sunsprite
Iceberg	Trumpeter

❋ *The first floribunda variety was introduced in 1922.*

Grandiflora Roses

'Grandiflora' means 'large flowers.' These roses have big flowers in small clusters. Grandiflora roses are the result of crosses between hybrid tea and floribunda roses, with the best qualities of both: magnificent, long-stemmed flowers and a profusion of blooms. Grandifloras have longer flower stems than floribundas; their rosebuds and flowers resemble those of the hybrid teas, and are good for cutting.

Flower colours are simple—for example, there are no lavenders to date and few mixed colours. Grandiflora roses tend to be taller than most hybrid teas, and up to twice the height of floribundas.

Favourite Grandiflora Roses

Aquarius
Gold Medal
Pink Parfait

Queen Elizabeth
Sonia

The first grandiflora rose was the variety Queen Elizabeth introduced in 1954.

Queen Elizabeth

Great Rosarians
Stewart Parker has a passion for rose stamps. Here he displays part of his collection from around the world.

Hybrid Tea Roses

Hybrid tea roses have large flowers and long, pointed flowerbuds, and generally produce one bloom per stem. These roses are the type usually sold by florists. The size of these rosebushes and the colour and fragrance of their flowers vary tremendously. Hybrid tea roses have the widest colour range, including many different blends and bicolours. They bloom almost continuously on long, straight stems, making them good garden shrubs as well as popular cutflowers.

Hybrid tea roses are the most popular type of rose in the world. The first variety was La France, introduced in 1867. It is rarely grown today, because of the wide selection of newer, improved varieties.

Favourite Hybrid Tea Roses

Dainty Bess	Olympiad
Double Delight	Painted Moon
Electron	Paradise
Elina	Pascali
Elizabeth Taylor	Paul Shirville
First Prize	Peace
Folklore	Pristine
Fragrant Cloud	Royal Highness
Garden Party	St. Patrick
Granada	Secret
Miss All-American Beauty	Tiffany
Mister Lincoln	Touch of Class

Electron derives its name from its hot pink colour.

Miniature Roses

Miniature roses look like smaller versions of hybrid tea roses, and most varieties bloom all summer. The size of miniature rosebushes varies from about 6 inches to 2 feet (15–60 cm) tall. Miniature roses are ideal for patio pots, edging, or even a low hedge. Most varieties have little to no fragrance.

Miniature roses may be brought indoors as a house-plant for a sunny location.

Favourite Miniature Roses

Cupcake	Rainbow's End
Little Artist	Rise 'n' Shine
Loving Touch	Snow Bride
Magic Carrousel	Starina
Minnie Pearl	Winsome

During the 18th and 19th centuries, miniature roses were known as 'fairy roses.'

The flowers of miniature roses can be as tiny as a fingernail or as large as a silver dollar.

PANACHE OF WILD GREENS ROSE PETAL VINAIGRETTE

Rose Petals (4 Red Roses)
1 Cup Champagne Vinegar
 or White Wine Vinegar
1 Tablespoon Honey
6 Tablespoons Olive Oil
$^1/_2$ Teaspoon (5 grams) Chopped Thyme
$^1/_2$ Teaspoon (5 grams) Chopped Rosemary

Method

Soak rose petals in vinegar and allow to infuse in sealed jar for 2 days. Strain petals out and add honey. Whisk together, and add olive oil and finely chopped herbs. Set aside.

To Finish

Wash baby wild greens, fold in vinaigrette, and sprinkle with multi-coloured rose petals.

Chef Raymond Taylor, of Edmonton's Hotel Macdonald, uses rose petals to make his panache of wild greens with a rose petal vinaigrette.

Abraham Darby

English Rose

It's a pretty strong statement for someone who has devoted himself to growing roses for the past dozen or more years, and who at the moment has over 250 different rose varieties in his garden, to name a variety that he wouldn't be without—but that's how Stephen Raven feels about Abraham Darby. The gorgeous colour and large size of the blooms are two of his reasons, but there is also its strong, sweet, fruity fragrance. Each rounded flower is large enough to fill the palm of your hand.

Official Colour •
  coppery apricot
Form • double
Scent • rich, fruity
ARS rating • (—)
Height •
  4–5 feet (1.2–1.5 m)
Spread •
  3 ¹/₂–4 feet (1–1.2 m)
Blooms • repeatedly
  from early summer
  to frost

TIPS

❋ Plant this dense, rounded shrub under a window that is often open, so that you can enjoy its fragrance from inside the house.

❋ Abraham Darby blooms with few breaks all summer. Its flowers are at least 4 to 4 ¹/₂ inches (10–11 cm) across, in a coppery apricot hue that fades to a pleasing soft pink on the outer petals.

❋ These roses are wonderful in bouquets. For the longest lasting flowers, cut just as the buds open. Be sure to include a few of the dark green, waxy leaves to offset the flower colour.

❋ This variety was introduced in 1985. Its namesake was a founder of the Industrial Revolution.

Abraham Darby is a superb rose with highly fragrant, very double, large, full flowers all summer.

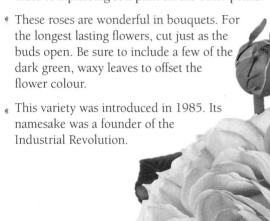

Apricot Nectar

Floribunda Rose

Official Colour •
   pink-apricot with
   golden base
Form • double
Scent • very fruity
ARS rating • 8.2
Height • 2–2 1/2 feet
   (60–75 cm)
Spread • 2–2 1/2 feet
   (60–75 cm)
Blooms • repeatedly
   from early summer
   to frost

Apricot Nectar is one of the smallest floribunda bushes, but its flowers are as large as those of most hybrid tea roses.

Customers at our greenhouses often stop to exclaim over Apricot Nectar's beauty. Its pastel flowers, strong perfume and small size are instantly endearing, but one of this variety's best features is not as immediately obvious. Once it is planted in your garden, you will soon discover that Apricot Nectar is one of the toughest roses, rarely bothered by disease, insects, heat or humidity.

TIPS

* Dark glossy foliage offsets the clusters of apricot flowers. This variety blooms repeatedly, most abundantly in midsummer.

* Each rose is 4 to 4 1/2 inches (10–11 cm) across, with multiple flowers in tight clusters. I like this effect, but some gardeners prefer to have one large flower per stem. To do this, remove all but the largest, central flowerbud while still in the bud stage.

* Apricot Nectar was introduced in 1965 and won the AARS award the following year.

Aquarius

Grandiflora Rose

A quarius is a very pretty rose that inspires beautiful bouquets. Dark pink rosebuds open to large flowers, from 3 1/2 to 4 1/2 inches (8.5–11 cm) across, in radiant shades of pink with a tint of lavender, and a bright yellow glow at the centre. Usually there is only one flower per stem, but sometimes you'll find small clusters. The flower colour holds well in hot weather.

TIPS

* These roses make long-lasting cutflowers. For best results, cut when rosebuds are loose but not fully open. Bouquets generally last 7 to 10 days.

* This variety has excellent disease resistance.

* Aquarius was introduced in 1971, and won the AARS award that year, as well as the Geneva Gold Medal in 1970.

Official Colour •
  pink blend
Form • double
Scent • light
ARS rating • 8.0
Height • 3–4 feet
  (90–120 cm)
Spread • 2 1/2–3 feet
  (75–90 cm)
Blooms • repeatedly
  from early summer
  to frost

Aquarius blooms profusely with large, long–stemmed flowers that are excellent for cutting.

Charles Austin

English Rose

TENDER

170

Official Colour • apricot
Form • double
Scent • strong, fruity
ARS rating • 8.2
Height • 3–4 feet
(90–120 cm)
Spread • 2¹/₂–3 feet
(75–90 cm)
Blooms • repeatedly
from early summer
to frost

Fragrant Charles Austin blooms in a stunning blend of soft pastel shades.

Charles Austin is one of those roses that draws people over for a closer look, and to sniff the fat flowers. The fragrance is strong and somewhat reminiscent of fresh fruit. These very full, 3- to 3¹/₂-inch (7.5–8.5 cm) flowers are borne one to a stem or in clusters of up to seven. The soft shades of apricot-yellow fade to pale pink, resulting in several different colours at once on the rosebush. Expect most flowers in early summer and fewer thereafter.

Tips

* Deadhead and fertilize regularly to encourage a stronger second flush of flowers. This variety does not always bloom well after its first flush.

* Cut these lovely, cup-shaped flowers for fragrant bouquets. Take as little of the stem as possible and use in a short vase or rosebowl.

* Charles Austin is susceptible to powdery mildew. To help prevent this disease, water in the morning rather than at night, and don't crowd the plants; good air circulation helps ward the disease off.

* This variety was introduced in 1973 and was named after breeder David Austin's father.

Charles Rennie Mackintosh

English Rose

Official Colour •
  pink blend
Form • double
Scent • very fragrant
ARS rating • (—)
Height • 3–3 1/2 feet
  (90–105 cm)
Spread • 2 1/2 feet
  (75 cm)
Blooms • continuously
  from early summer
  to frost

Charles Rennie Mackintosh has full, rounded flowers that look like peonies. Unlike peonies, however, these roses bloom all summer. Their frilly, 2 1/2- to 3-inch (6–7.5 cm) flowers vary in colour—ranging from pink to dusty lilac to pure lilac—depending on age and weather. The fragrance is remarkable. This is a vigorous, bushy shrub with dark green leaves and lots of flowers on thorny, wiry stems.

TIPS

❋ These fragrant flowers look astounding in bouquets or floating in rosebowls. Push their thorns sideways with your thumb to remove them from the branches.

❋ This rose is a tough and reliable variety. Its breeding background includes a rugosa rose, which provides improved hardiness and disease resistance.

❋ Charles Rennie Mackintosh was introduced in 1988. Its namesake is a famous Art Nouveau designer and architect.

❋ *Charles Rennie Mackintosh has fat, fragrant flowers all summer in a distinctive shade of dusty lilac.*

Miniature Rose

TENDER

Official Colour •
medium pink
Form • double
Scent • little to none
ARS rating • 8.5
Height • 12–14 inches
(30–35 cm)
Spread • 12–14 inches
(30–35 cm)
Blooms • continuously
from early summer
to frost

Cupcake

Cupcake is an irresistible miniature rose. Perfect little flowers in the classic hybrid tea shape cover this neat, rounded bush, making a charming display in patio pots throughout summer. The plants are bushy, vigorous and undemanding, with lovely glossy foliage, no prickles and salmon-pink flowers that look good enough to eat.

Tips

❀ Cupcake blooms non-stop all summer, with 1 ½-inch (3.5 cm) flowers borne one to a stem or in clusters of up to five.

❀ Remove finished flowers to keep plants tidy and encourage more blooms.

❀ This disease-resistant variety was introduced in 1981, and it won the ARS Award of Excellence for Miniature Roses in 1983.

✤ *Cupcake is the one of the best miniature roses, with lots of very full, double flowers.*

Dainty Bess

Hybrid Tea Rose

Dainty Bess stands out in a crowd. Its flowers have five silky, silvery-pink, ruffled petals offset by striking burgundy stamens—an unusual feature as 90 percent of roses have yellow stamens. The flowers are 3 1/2 inches (8.5 cm) across, and may appear either one to a stem or in clusters. For 60 years, Dainty Bess reigned as the most popular single-flowered hybrid tea rose.

Official Colour • light pink
Form • single
Scent • light 'tea rose' fragrance
ARS rating • 9.0
Height • 2–2 1/2 feet (60–75 cm)
Spread • 2 feet (60 cm)
Blooms • repeatedly, all summer to frost

TIPS

* Depending on the amount of sun they receive and where they appear on the bush, flowers have various hues, from dusty pink to almost white.

* This sturdy, upright bush has leathery, disease-resistant foliage and few thorns. It is hardier than many hybrid teas, although plants still need winter protection (see page 62).

* I wouldn't cut this rose for bouquets, because the flowers are not long lasting, and have the habit of closing at night, which is unusual for a rose.

* Dainty Bess was introduced in 1925, and won the Royal National Rose Society Gold Medal the same year. At one time, this variety was promoted as 'The Artistic Rose,' an apparent reference to its beautiful, distinctive flowers.

Dainty Bess is one of the oldest and most unusual hybrid tea roses still available today.

Hybrid Tea Rose

TENDER

Official Colour •
red blend
Form • double
Scent • very strong,
spicy
ARS rating • 8.9
Height • 3 ¹/₂–4 feet
(1–1.2 m)
Spread • 2–2 ¹/₂ feet
(60–75 cm)
Blooms • repeatedly, all
season to frost

Double Delight

The first time I saw a photograph of Double Delight, I was sure someone was playing tricks. This variety has captivating flowers that look as if they had been painted like the roses in *Alice in Wonderland*. These huge flowers, each up to 5 ¹/₂ inches (13.5 cm) across, change from creamy white edged in red to almost solid strawberry red. No two colour patterns are ever the same. As an added bonus, this variety is one of the most fragrant roses.

TIPS

* Because of the wide red rim outlining each flower, the French call this variety La Rose de Rouge à Lèvres: the Lipstick Rose.

* Flower colours change with the weather. In cool temperatures, flowers are quite white with a red rim, but when it's hot and as flowers age, they tend to be redder.

* This variety can be susceptible to powdery mildew. To help prevent it, water in the morning rather than at night, and don't crowd the plants; good air circulation helps ward off this disease.

* Although Double Delight is less hardy in northern gardens than many hybrid tea roses, plants thrive for years if provided with proper winter protection. Our rosebush is now over 10 years old.

Introduced in 1977, Double Delight has won the 1976 Rome Gold Medal, 1976 Baden-Baden Gold Medal, 1977 AARS, 1986 James Alexander Gamble Rose Fragrance Award and the 1986 ARS Fragrance Award. This variety was named 'World's Favourite Rose' in 1985.

What are the two most delightful things about Double Delight? One, it has unique, bicoloured flowers, and two, it has an award–winning perfume.

Electron

Hybrid Tea Rose

You can't miss Electron in the garden. The flowers are brilliant hot pink, very fragrant and huge—up to 5 inches (12.5 cm) across! This variety blooms abundantly, and both the flowers and flowerbuds are long lasting, providing a magnificent display with few breaks in bloom throughout the season. Plant Electron in a prominent site where it is handy to pause and inhale its sweet perfume.

Official Colour •
  dark pink
Form • double
Scent • strong sweet-rose
  fragrance
ARS rating • 7.7
Height • 2¹/₂–3 feet
  (75–90 cm)
Spread • 2–2¹/₂ feet
  (60–75 cm)
Blooms • repeatedly
  from early summer
  to frost

TIPS

❀ Avoid planting in hot sites near heat-reflecting brick or stucco walls. Electron prefers more moderate temperatures.

❀ Snip flowers to float in rosebowls for a fragrant and impressive display. These very full roses have fairly long stems and also make good cutflowers.

❀ This variety has excellent disease resistance.

❀ Introduced in 1970, Electron went on to win many awards, including The Hague Gold Medal in 1970, Belfast Gold Medal in 1972, AARS in 1973 and Portland Gold Medal in 1973.

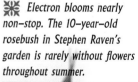

Electron blooms nearly non–stop. The 10–year–old rosebush in Stephen Raven's garden is rarely without flowers throughout summer.

Elina

Hybrid Tea Rose

Official Colour •
light yellow
Form • double
Scent • light, fruity
ARS rating • 8.6
Height • 3–3 1/2 feet
(90–105 cm)
Spread • 2–2 1/2 feet
(60–75 cm)
Blooms • repeatedly
from early summer
to frost

Elina is a lovely pale yellow rosebush that holds its colour well and is usually in bloom.

With more flowers than many other hybrid tea roses, Elina is a marvellous variety for cutflowers. Its long-stemmed, 3 1/2- to 4-inch (8.5–10 cm), double flowers last well in bouquets, and their luminescent soft yellow colour is offset by large, deep green, glossy leaves. This variety is rain tolerant, which means the petals don't show unsightly marks after a summer shower. Elina is often called one of the world's best roses.

TIPS

※ Elina has great heat tolerance, but its flowers are larger in cool conditions. For best results, avoid planting in a flowerbed against a south-facing wall. An open bed permits cooling breezes and better air circulation, which will also help prevent powdery mildew.

※ This Irish variety was introduced in 1984, and won both the ADR Gold Medal and New Zealand Gold Star in 1987. It is sometimes known as Peaudouce, which means 'soft skin' in French, referring to the silky petals.

Elizabeth Taylor

Hybrid Tea Rose

Official Colour •
  dark pink
Form • double
Scent • spicy
ARS rating • 8.8
Height • 3–3 1/2 feet
  (90–105 cm)
Spread • 3–3 1/2 feet
  (90–105 cm)
Blooms • continuously
  from early summer
  to frost

I magine inviting friends over to see Elizabeth Taylor in your own backyard. We once did a playful advertising campaign with the Elizabeth Taylor rose, and three years later customers still recall those ads and ask for 'Liz' by name. These flowers are very large, full and fragrant, similar to those of Mister Lincoln, except in colour. Elizabeth Taylor is rich, deep lavender-pink with darker edges. Count on a profusion of lovely, long-lived flowers throughout the season.

TIPS

* Plant this variety in a site that is sunny but not hot. Flowers may be smaller in the heat of summer.

* Elizabeth Taylor is so productive that you'll have plenty of exhibition-quality flowers to cut for impressive bouquets. These flowers are 4 to 4 1/2 inches (10–11 cm) across, and there is usually one to each long stem. The foliage is rich and semi-glossy.

* To help prevent powdery mildew, water in the morning rather than at night, and don't crowd the plants; good air circulation helps ward off this disease.

* This variety was introduced in 1986.

Elizabeth Taylor is a star performer, with lots and lots of huge, plump, fragrant flowers on its long stems.

English Garden

Official Colour • apricot
Form • double
Scent • light 'tea rose'
  fragrance
ARS rating • 7.9
Height • 3–3 1/2 feet
  (90–105 cm)
Spread • 2 1/2–3 feet
  (75–90 cm)
Blooms • repeatedly
  from early summer
  to frost

English Garden is a rose that will draw passersby into your garden for a closer look at its impressive flowers. The 3 1/2-inch (8.5 cm) flowers are buff-yellow in the centre, with outer petals ranging from soft apricot to creamy white in colour. Pale green leaves offset the flower colour. Like old-fashioned roses, these flowers are flattened and quartered—very full with hundreds of small, tightly packed petals. The fragrance is wonderful, although not terribly strong.

TIPS

* With its small, compact form, English Garden fits easily into most flowerbeds or borders.

* These pastel-coloured flowers are irresistible, and a must for cutting to display in bouquets or rosebowls.

* Deadhead regularly until a few weeks before the end of summer to encourage further blooming.

* This variety was introduced in 1986.

English Garden has very full flowers like the old garden roses, but unlike those varieties, it blooms all summer.

Escapade

Escapade is almost always covered in flowers. It begins its show a bit later than other roses, but produces lots of flowers while many rose varieties slow down or take a break in blooming. For the rest of the season, Escapade blooms almost constantly. The rose-violet, 3-inch (7.5 cm) flowers have snowy white centres, and are borne in big, beautiful clusters. This variety is sometimes described as semi-double, because it has twice as many petals as most single roses.

Official Colour • mauve blend

TENDER

Form • single

Scent • musk-rose fragrance

ARS rating • 8.8

Height • 2 1/2–3 feet (75–90 cm)

Spread • 2–2 1/2 feet (60–75 cm)

Blooms • repeatedly from early summer to frost

TIPS

❀ Escapade is shade tolerant, and it blooms well even with only a half day of sun. It also has excellent resistance to powdery mildew and blackspot.

❀ This bushy variety makes a splendid addition to mixed borders, because it doesn't have bare lower stems as do some of the other floribunda roses.

❀ For the longest-lasting bouquets, cut these flowers before they are fully open.

❀ This variety is one of the bigger and most winter-hardy floribundas, although it still requires winter protection (see page 62).

❀ Escapade was introduced in 1967, and in 1969 won the Belfast Gold Medal, the Baden-Baden Gold Medal and the ADR award.

Escapade is one of the most free-flowering floribundas, with a profusion of flowers in big clusters throughout the season.

Europeana

Official Colour •
dark red
Form • double
Scent • light 'tea rose'
fragrance
ARS rating • 9.0
Height • 2¹/₂–3 feet
(75–90 cm)
Spread • 2–3 feet
(60–90 cm)
Blooms • repeatedly
from early summer
to frost

When Europeana blooms, you can barely see its foliage. Huge clusters of dark crimson, semi-double to double flowers absolutely cover this bush. The cupped flowers are 3 inches (7.5 cm) across, with thick, almost waxy petals. New leaves are red, changing to glossy bronze-green. This variety begins blooming a little later than many varieties, providing a splendid show of midseason colour. Europeana is a superb red rose with unfading colour.

TIPS

* Europeana likes heat. Even in a hot, sunny flowerbed, the long-lasting flowers hold their colour without fading.

* This variety can be susceptible to powdery mildew. To help prevent it, water in morning rather than at night, and provide plants with good air circulation.

* Although hardier than many floribundas, Europeana still needs to be provided with winter protection (see page 62).

* Europeana was introduced in 1963, and won The Hague Gold Medal in 1962, AARS in 1968 and the Portland Gold Medal in 1970.

Europeana seems to bloom forever, with masses of long–lasting flowers in huge, heavy clusters.

Evelyn

E velyn is one of the best-known English roses, and gardeners ask for it specifically. It is named for the British perfume company Crabtree & Evelyn, which chose this rose to represent its business. Evelyn is a magnificent rose, with lots of 4-inch (10 cm) apricot and yellow flowers tinged in pink, and a powerful fragrance that is both sweet and fruity. It blooms on and off throughout summer.

Tips

* For the best flower colour, avoid planting in extremely hot areas of the garden. Evelyn's flowers tend to fade in heat, and to turn pinker towards the end of summer.

* Evelyn blooms with small clusters of satiny-petalled flowers. Just one cluster in a vase will fill a room with incredible perfume.

* This rose can be susceptible to blackspot. Avoid wetting its foliage and water at the base of the plant rather than from overhead, to reduce blackspot problems.

* Evelyn was introduced in 1991. Its complex fragrance includes 84 different chemicals, among them, surprisingly, acetone and benzene.

English Rose

Official Colour • apricot
Form • double
Scent • extremely fragrant
ARS rating • 7.6
Height • 3–3 1/2 feet (90–105 cm)
Spread • 3 feet (90 cm)
Blooms • repeatedly from early summer to frost

Almost all English roses are noted for their scent, but creator David Austin cites Evelyn as having the strongest, most delicious fragrance of all his varieties!

Floribunda Rose

Eyepaint

TENDER

182

Official Colour •
   red blend
Form • single
Scent • light
ARS rating • 8.1
Height • 2–3 feet
   (60–90 cm)
Spread • 2–2 1/2 feet
   (60–75 cm)
Blooms • repeatedly
   from early summer
   to frost

I love Eyepaint's distinctive, rather unrose-like flowers. The ruffled petals are tipped bright scarlet and surround white and yellow centres. The effect of these staring 'eyes' is startling from a distance, but take a close look at the flowers to discover how this variety gained its name. Eyepaint is termed a 'handpainted' rose, because it looks as if an artist had quickly brushed red paint across the white petals. Eyepaint was the first widely available handpainted rose.

TIPS

* Remove the entire cluster after flowering to encourage new blooms. Stop deadheading a few weeks before the end of summer, to allow the plant to slow down growth in preparation for winter.

* Because this variety can be susceptible to blackspot, be sure to water plants at the base rather than from overhead.

* This rose is one of the hardiest floribundas, with a bushy form and flowers that stand up well to all sorts of weather.

* This award-winning variety was considered to be a breeding break-through when it was introduced in 1975.

My granddaughter loves looking at Eyepaint's flowers; they remind her of the scene in Disney's animated version of Alice in Wonderland, when the white roses were painted red to appease the Queen of Hearts.

Fair Bianca

Fair Bianca blooms profusely in early summer with fat rosebuds tinged in pink, opening to exquisite, 4-inch (10 cm), pure white flowers. The fragrance is intense and rather uncommon; the old-fashioned myrrh fragrance is not often found in newer varieties. This rose looks somewhat like the damask rose Mme. Hardy, with similar cupped flowers and tightly packed petals around a central green button. Fair Bianca is a bushy, upright plant with light green leaves and many small thorns.

Official Colour • white
Form • double
Scent • strong myrrh
  fragrance
ARS rating • 8.2
Height • 3–3 1/2 feet
  (90–105 cm)
Spread • 2–2 1/2 feet
  (60–75 cm)
Blooms • repeatedly
  from early summer
  to frost

TENDER

183

TIPS

❀ Fair Bianca is what we call a 'self-cleaning' rose. Petals fall cleanly from finished flowers, resulting in a tidier bush, although deadheading is still required if you want more blooms.

❀ To encourage repeat flowering, be sure to fertilize and deadhead regularly. Fair Bianca is somewhat particular and doesn't always re-bloom well in less than ideal conditions.

❀ This variety was introduced in 1982. It is one of the most disease-resistant English roses.

Fair Bianca is one of the most fragrant and beautiful white roses.

First Edition

Official Colour •
orange-pink
Form • double
Scent • light 'tea rose'
fragrance
ARS rating • 8.6
Height • 2½–3 feet
(75–90 cm)
Spread • 2 feet
(60 cm)
Blooms • continuously
from early summer
to frost

Coral is becoming a popular colour for flowers, and gardeners who like matching their flowers are overjoyed to discover a rose in this shade. First Edition begins blooming a little later than some roses, providing a midseason splash of colour with luminous coral flowers that are tinged neon orange, pink and red. These lovely flowers are 2 to 2½ inches (5–6 cm) across, borne one to a stem and in clusters, and they glow against glossy, light green leaves.

TIPS

❀ For larger flowers and stronger colour, plant this rose in a bed that is sunny but not excessively hot.

❀ Cut these flowers often for bouquets. First Edition has strong, upright stems and makes a good cutflower.

❀ To encourage blooming, remove the entire cluster after flowering.

❀ This variety was introduced in 1976, and won the AARS award the following year. It is sometimes listed as Arnaud Delbard (the name of the breeder).

First Edition is an unusual colour for a rose—bright coral with vibrant shades of orange, red and pink.

First Prize

First Prize easily wins hearts with its stunning flowers. Every year when this variety sells out at our greenhouses, customers ask to be put on a waiting list for next year. Huge pointed rosebuds open to stunning, 5-inch (12.5 cm) flowers in shades of ivory to soft shimmering pink, with darker edges. First Prize produces fewer flowers than some varieties, but each flower is perfection in itself.

Official Colour • pink blend
Form • double
Scent • mild 'tea rose' fragrance
ARS rating • 8.9
Height • 2–2 1/2 feet (60–75 cm)
Spread • 3 feet (90 cm)
Blooms • repeatedly from early summer to frost

TIPS

* Have patience with young plants. This variety may bloom sparsely for the first year or two after planting.

* Unfortunately, this beautiful rose is prone to both blackspot and mildew. To prevent these diseases, don't crowd the plants. Water in the morning rather than at night, and direct your spray at the base of the plant to avoid wetting the foliage.

* These long-stemmed roses are wonderful for lasting bouquets. Cut at the tight rosebud stage for the longest vase life.

* First Prize was the last rose produced by the famous American rose breeder Gene Boerner. It was introduced in 1970, won the AARS award the same year and the ARS Gold Medal in 1971.

First Prize lives up to its name—this variety has been the top-rated exhibition rose in the United States for over a decade!

Official Colour •
  dark red
Form • double
Scent • strong 'old rose'
  fragrance
ARS rating • 8.0
Height • 3 1/2–4 feet
  (1–1.2 m)
Spread • 2 1/2–3 feet
  (75–90 cm)
Blooms • repeatedly
  from early summer
  to frost

Fisherman's Friend

Fisherman's Friend has dark crimson flowers the colour of garnets, with lighter undersides and a powerful perfume. As flowers age, their colour changes to cherry red or crimson-purple, creating several shades of red on the rosebush at one time. The 3-inch (7.5 cm) flowers are very full, borne one to a stem or in heavy clusters of three or more. This is a stunning rose, with very dark foliage. It blooms profusely in early summer and again in fall.

TIPS

❀ The weight of these heavy flowers can cause branches to bow down. If you don't like this effect, plant these rosebushes near a fence or pillar to which you can attach the canes.

❀ Cut these beautiful flowers for bouquets, but handle with care, as the stems are covered with wicked thorns. Just one cluster of flowers fills a room with evocative perfume.

❀ Unfortunately, this lovely rose is susceptible to both blackspot and powdery mildew. Wet foliage encourages disease, so be sure to just water the soil around the plants and avoid the foliage. Water in the morning rather than at night, and provide the plants with good air circulation.

❀ *Fisherman's Friend has very dark, full, fragrant flowers.*

❀ This rose is one of the hardier English roses, surviving cold winters easily when provided with protection.

❀ Fisherman's Friend was introduced in 1987. It was named at an auction on behalf of the British charity 'Children in Need.'

Folklore

With its fragrant, coral-orange flowers, glossy, coppery-green foliage and tan prickles, Folklore adds a different hue to the garden. These high-centred, double flowers are large, about 4 ½ inches (11 cm) across, very full and nicely scented. The orange petals are paler on the undersides, creating quite a charming effect. I like to offset the colour of these flowers in bouquets with blue speedwell and white astilbe.

Official Colour •
  orange blend
Form • double
Scent • fragrant
ARS rating • 8.5
Height •
  5–6 feet (1.5–1.8 m)
Spread •
  3 ½–4 feet (1–1.2 m)
Blooms • repeatedly
  from early summer
  to frost

TIPS

❋ Plant Folklore at the back of the border, where it provides a lovely backdrop to shorter shrubs and flowers.

❋ Deadhead regularly throughout summer to encourage further blooming. Stop deadheading a few weeks before the end of summer to allow plants to slow their growth down before winter arrives.

❋ This vigorous, upright variety was introduced in 1977.

Folklore is one of the tallest hybrid tea roses.

Hybrid Tea Rose

Fragrant Cloud

TENDER

Official Colour •
orange-red
Form • double
Scent • exceptionally
strong
ARS rating • 8.3
Height • 3–4 feet
(90–120 cm)
Spread • 3–3 1/2 feet
(90–105 cm)
Blooms • repeatedly
from early summer
to frost

Fragrant Cloud is a rose many gardeners tell me they wouldn't be without. Its intense perfume fills the garden and with the slightest breeze, wafts indoors through open windows. The scent ranges from spicy clove to sweet rose, and is extremely powerful. The Vancouver Rose Society actually separates this variety from their list of fragrant roses, putting Fragrant Cloud in a class of its own. There are many fragrant roses, but Fragrant Cloud floats high above them all.

TIPS

❋ Just one cutflower fills an entire room with breathtaking perfume!

❋ Flower colour tends to fade rather quickly. The colour is deepest in cooler weather.

❋ As this variety can be susceptible to blackspot, water in the morning rather than in the evening, and direct your spray at the plant's base to avoid wetting the foliage.

❋ Since it was introduced in 1967, Fragrant Cloud has won numerous awards, including the Royal National Rose Society's President's International Trophy in 1964, Portland Gold Medal in 1966, Rose of the Year in 1986 and James Alexander Gamble Rose Fragrance Award in 1969.

❋ The brilliant orange-red colour of these 5-inch (12.5 cm), double roses reminds me of geraniums, one of my all-time favourite flowers.

❋ Fragrant Cloud was also honoured by being named 'World's Favourite Rose' by the World Federation of Rose Societies in 1981. This variety is sometimes listed as Duftwolke or Nuage Perfume.

Garden Party

Hybrid Tea Rose

With its large, double flowers in shades of pale yellow to ivory, and its petal tips dabbed in pink, Garden Party defies its official colour designation of 'white.' It looks like a paler version of its parent Peace, the world's most famous rose. Each of Garden Party's flowers is 4 to 5 inches (10–12.5 cm) across, with a lovely but faint perfume. This variety blooms most profusely in midsummer, with fewer flowers until frost. Dark green leaves with reddish undersides offset the graceful flowers.

Official Colour • white
Form • double
Scent • light 'tea rose' fragrance
ARS rating • 8.2
Height • 3 feet (90 cm)
Spread • 2 feet (60 cm)
Blooms • repeatedly from early summer to frost

TENDER

TIPS

* Garden Party produces the most flowers when it is grown in full sun. Choose a site that is warm but not hot to prevent the flower colour from fading.

* In cool temperatures, the petals can be quite pink. Flowers are paler in hot weather, but never without a faint tinge of pink. Fall flowers tend to be darker.

* Garden Party can be susceptible to powdery mildew. To help prevent it, water in the morning rather than at night, and don't crowd the plants; good air circulation helps ward off the disease.

* This variety is one of the older hybrid teas, introduced in 1959. Garden Party won the Bagatelle Gold Medal in 1959 and was an AARS winner in 1960.

Garden Party is a beautiful rose, with large flowers in delicate pastel colours.

Gene Boerner

Floribunda Rose

Official Colour •
medium pink
Form • double
Scent • light, sweet
ARS rating • 8.5
Height • 2–2 ¹/₂ feet
(60–75 cm)
Spread • 2–2 ¹/₂ feet
(60–75 cm)
Blooms • repeatedly
from early summer
to frost

Gene Boerner is a true pink rose, with pure colour spread evenly across its petals. These double flowers are 3 to 3 ¹/₂ inches (7.5–8.5 cm) across, and appear one to a stem or in clusters. They look like hybrid tea roses, and stand out well against dark, glossy foliage on a bushy, upright shrub. Gene Boerner produces lots of flowers—more than most floribundas—and has a gentle but lovely old-fashioned fragrance.

TIPS

* When temperatures cool in fall, these roses may take on a darker hue.

* Gene Boerner has few thorns, which makes it easy to cut flowers for bouquets.

* Introduced in 1968, this variety was named after the American rose breeder who is often credited with having contributed more towards the development of floribundas than any other rose breeder. This rose won the AARS award in 1969.

Gene Boerner blooms profusely with long–lasting, pure pink flowers.

Gertrude Jekyll

English Rose

Gertrude Jekyll can really surprise you. It seems unbelievable that such tiny rosebuds can produce such large, full flowers. Rich, deep pink petals spiral from the centres, forming very full, powerfully fragrant, 3 ½- to 4-inch (8.5–10 cm) wide flowers, in small clusters. In England, this rose is now grown commercially for perfume—the first time in about 250 years that English farmers have raised roses for this purpose. Gertrude Jekyll's flowers tend to be darker, almost red, in cool weather.

Official Colour •
  medium pink
Form • double
Scent • very strong,
  sweet
ARS rating • (—)
Height •
  4–5 feet (1.2–1.5 m)
Spread •
  3–4 feet (90–120 cm)
Blooms • repeatedly
  from early summer
  to frost

TIPS

❋ I can never resist snipping these fragrant flowers for bouquets or rosebowls.

❋ Gertrude Jekyll can be susceptible to powdery mildew. To help prevent it, water in the morning rather than at night, and don't crowd the plants; good air circulation helps ward off this disease.

❋ Although winter protection is recommended, this variety is quite a hardy rose. In our garden it has leafed out on branches above the snowline even after winter temperatures of -22° F (-30° C).

❋ This variety was introduced in 1986. It is named after a famous English gardener and author. The name is pronounced JEE-kul, unlike the name of Mr. Hyde's alter-ego.

❋❋ *English roses are among the most fragrant of all roses, and Gertrude Jekyll is one of the most strongly scented roses in its class.*

Glamis Castle

Official Colour • white
Form • double
Scent • strong
ARS rating • (—)
Height • 3 feet
(90 cm)
Spread • 2 ½–3 feet
(75–90 cm)
Blooms • repeatedly
from early summer
to frost

TENDER

Glamis Castle blooms like a floribunda, with its abundant, very fragrant flowers throughout summer and only brief breaks between peak periods of bloom. The white flowers are 2 ½ to 3 inches (6–7.5 cm) across, and very full, with about 200 petals! Occasionally, flowers have a hint of buff in their centres when they first open. The scent is described as myrrh, a distinctive, delicious, spicy mixture of scents that has become rare in roses.

TIPS

* Plant this short, bushy rose in a flowerbed near a walkway or garden bench, so that you are able to enjoy its potent scent. Glamis Castle is an ideal size for small gardens.

* I love its fragrance, and often cut the flowers for bouquets, or snip off just a single bloom to float in a rosebowl.

* This variety was introduced in 1992. It is named after the childhood home of Her Majesty the Queen Mother and the birthplace of Princess Margaret. Glamis Castle is the setting for Shakespeare's *Macbeth*.

❋ *Glamis Castle is the best white English rose.*

Gold Medal

Gold Medal is a wonderful yellow rose, with long-lasting flowers in several different shades on the bush at one time. Golden-yellow rosebuds with tawny edges open to rich yellow-gold, 3 1/2-inch (8.5 cm) flowers that soften as they age to paler yellow with petals tipped in pink. Gold Medal blooms throughout the season, with abundant waves of flowers that provide a stunning display in the garden and in bouquets.

Official Colour • medium yellow
Form • double
Scent • light 'tea rose' fragrance
ARS rating • 8.8
Height • 3–4 feet (90–120 cm)
Spread • 2–3 feet (60–90 cm)
Blooms • repeatedly from early summer to frost

TIPS

* Grandiflora roses tend to bloom both with flowers one to a stem and in clusters. Gold Medal produces more single-stemmed roses than most grandiflora varieties.

* Although more disease resistant than many yellow roses, this variety may occasionally get blackspot. To help prevent this fungal disease, avoid wetting the foliage. Water at the base of the plant rather than from overhead.

* Cut these lovely flowers for long-lasting bouquets.

* Gold Medal is one of the hardiest grandifloras, but it still requires winter protection as recommended on page 62.

* This variety was introduced in 1982, and, living up to its name, won the New Zealand Gold Medal in 1983.

Gold Medal is the best yellow grandiflora, with scads of large, fragrant flowers.

Graham Thomas

English Rose

Official Colour •
  dark yellow
Form • double
Scent • rich 'tea rose'
  fragrance
ARS rating • 7.9
Height •
  4–5 feet (1.2–1.5 cm)
Spread •
  3–4 feet (90–120 cm)
Blooms • continuously
  from early summer
  to frost

Graham Thomas may very well be the best known and most popular English rose. It blooms non-stop from early summer to fall, in an unmatched shade of sunny, rich butter yellow, with fragrant flowers that look like old garden roses. Apricot-pink rosebuds open to large flowers, from 4 to 5 inches (10–12.5 cm) across. Their colour softens pleasingly with age. These full roses make outstanding, though rather short-lived, cutflowers.

TIPS

* Avoid planting this rose in very hot areas of the garden, since heat causes fewer flowers and fast-fading colour. Graham Thomas has good disease resistance in gardens across the country.

* The flowers are unaffected by wet weather, but regular deadheading is required to prolong the flowering period.

* Although winter protection is recommended, this is quite a hardy rose. In our garden it has leafed out on branches above the snowline even after winter temperatures of -22° F (-30° C).

* This variety was introduced in 1983. Its namesake, Graham Stuart Thomas, is a popular, influential, British gardening authority and author.

Graham Thomas is the best yellow rose available today.

Granada

Before it even opens its first fragrant flower, Granada is easy to identify. This rose stands out in a crowd of other roses with its unusual, crinkled, holly-like leaves. When Granada blooms, however, you can't mistake it for any other variety. No other rose produces a similar profusion of high-centred, 4- to 5-inch (10–12.5 cm) flowers in intense shades of red, orange, pink and lemon-yellow. Granada is sometimes called 'the birthday cake rose' because its flowers look like the icing flowers that are used to decorate cakes.

Official Colour • red blend
Form • double
Scent • strong, spicy
ARS rating • 8.3
Height • 2 feet (60 cm)
Spread • 2 feet (60 cm)
Blooms • repeatedly from early summer to frost

TIPS

* Plant this rose in a protected site, against the foundation of a heated building on the south or west side. It is more tender than most hybrid roses.

* Granada has good resistance to blackspot, but it is susceptible to powdery mildew. To help prevent mildew, water in the morning rather than at night, and don't crowd the plants; good air circulation helps ward off the disease.

* Introduced in 1963, this rose was an AARS winner in 1964 and won the James Alexander Gamble Rose Fragrance Award in 1968, one of only nine roses to be so honoured in the last 35 years. It is also known as Donatella.

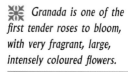
Granada is one of the first tender roses to bloom, with very fragrant, large, intensely coloured flowers.

Floribunda Rose

Official Colour •
   light pink
Form • very double
Scent • soft, sweet
ARS rating • 8.3
Height • 3–3¹/₂ feet
   (90–105 cm)
Spread • 2–2¹/₂ feet
   (60–75 cm)
Blooms • repeatedly
   from early summer
   to frost

*Gruss an Aachen is one
of the oldest floribundas still
readily available, with large,
old–fashioned–style, fully
double flowers all season.*

Gruss an Aachen

Gruss an Aachen is a bit of an oddity. It is listed as a floribunda, although it was introduced in 1909, 13 years before the floribunda class actually existed. Its clustered flowers, which look like old-fashioned roses, open to a tightly packed ball of up to 200 silky petals. (Most double roses have from 30 to 40 petals.) Orange-red and yellow rosebuds open to softly scented, peach-pink flowers that gently fade to creamy white. Against the rich green, leathery foliage, the flowers glow like pearls.

TIPS

* Gruss an Aachen is a dwarf, bushy shrub that looks lovely in containers. See page 43 for details on growing patio roses.

* This disease-resistant variety tolerates partial shade, but it does best in full sun and rich, well-drained soil.

* Almost a century after its introduction, Gruss an Aachen is still one of the most highly rated roses. Its name means 'Greetings from Aachen' (a city in western Germany on the Belgian border).

Heritage

Heritage has an intoxicating fragrance and irresistible, very full, shell-pink flowers. The 4-inch (10 cm), cupped flowers are borne one to a stem or in clusters of about four, and occasionally in very large clusters. Heritage's best feature, to me, is its perfume, which is very strong and heavy with delicious hints of honey and lemon. This is an upright, bushy plant with dark, semi-glossy leaves, few thorns and loads of flowers.

Official Colour • light pink
Form • double
Scent • very fragrant
ARS rating • 8.7
Height • 4–4 1/2 feet (1.2–1.4 m)
Spread • 3–3 1/2 feet (90–105 cm)
Blooms • repeatedly from early summer to frost

TENDER

TIPS

* Have patience with young plants. It may take two to three years after planting before your rosebush blooms profusely.

* Unfortunately, these flowers are short lived in the vase so they aren't the best roses for cutting. The large number of flowers in the garden makes up for this shortfall.

Heritage is among the most fragrant of all roses, with a unique lemony scent.

* Heritage is susceptible to blackspot. To help prevent this fungal disease, avoid wetting the foliage. Water at the base of the plant rather than from overhead.

* This variety was introduced in 1985.

Iceberg

Floribunda Rose

Official Colour • white
Form • double
Scent • very sweet
ARS rating • 8.7
Height • 4–4¹/₂ feet
   (1.2–1.4 m)
Spread • 3–4 feet
   (90–120 cm)
Blooms • continuously
   from early summer
   to frost

Iceberg is, without a doubt, one of the most popular roses in the world. Many gardeners who don't even grow roses know this one by name. Iceberg blooms profusely, with large clusters of fragrant, long-lasting, double flowers, each 3 inches (7.5 cm) across. It begins blooming early, and continues until stopped by fall frosts. Late season flowers often have a tinge of blush-pink. The World Federation of Rose Societies has named just eight roses as 'World's Favourite Rose,' including Iceberg in 1983 as the only floribunda.

TIPS

* Because it is one of the most winter-hardy floribundas, Iceberg has less dieback and subsequently gets taller than most other floribunda varieties. It flushes out into a nice, round bush, and it looks wonderful planted in a mixed flower garden.

* How long do tender roses live in northern gardens? Nobody seems to know the answer for certain, but our Iceberg rose is now 13 years old.

* That 13-year-old rose was mistakenly planted with its graft above the soil line, rather than buried—testament to Iceberg's cold-hardiness. We do, however, still recommend that you plant Iceberg in the same manner as other tender roses (see page 35).

* This variety was introduced in 1958, and won the Royal National Rose Society Gold Medal the same year. Almost 40 years later, Iceberg remains one of the top-rated roses. It is sometimes listed as Schneewittchen or Fee des Neiges.

Iceberg is the best of all the floribunda roses!

L.D. Braithwaite

English Rose

Official Colour •
  dark red
Form • double
Scent • 'old rose'
  fragrance
ARS rating • (—)
Height •
  3 1/2–4 feet (1–1.2 m)
Spread •
  3 1/2–4 feet (1–1.2 m)
Blooms • repeatedly
  from early summer
  to frost

TENDER

199

Almost everyone who sees L.D. Braithwaite falls in love with its sumptuous flowers, which are fragrant, 4 inches (10 cm) across and deep, rich crimson. The colour scarcely fades, holding better than almost all other red roses. This variety is one of our nursery manager Shane Neufeld's favourite English roses—in fact, it is one of the best-selling English roses in the world! Just one of L.D. Braithwaite's flowers makes an impressive display in a glass vase.

TIPS

* Flowers may be fewer and smaller on young plants, but a year or two after planting, L.D. Braithwaite blooms in full splendour.

* This rose makes a superb cutflower.

* L.D. Braithwaite has good resistance to blackspot, but can be susceptible to powdery mildew. To help prevent this fungal disease, water in the morning rather than at night, and don't crowd the plants; good air circulation helps ward it off.

* This variety was introduced in 1988. It is named after breeder David Austin's father-in-law.

❀ *L.D. Braithwaite is the brightest crimson of all English roses, and it is one of the best red roses, period!*

English Rose

Official Colour •
    orange-pink
Form • double
Scent • fragrant
ARS rating • 9.4
Height • 3–3 1/2 feet
    (90–105 cm)
Spread • 2 1/2–3 feet
    (75–90 cm)
Blooms • repeatedly
    from early summer
    to frost

Lilian Austin

Lilian Austin adds a nice blend of colours—salmon-pink flowers tinted apricot and pale orange—to the garden. These fragrant flowers are 3 1/2 inches (8.5 cm) across, with wavy petals that sometimes fold back to expose the stamens. Sometimes you will find one rose to a stem, and sometimes clusters of about five. This variety is a charming rosebush, with glossy dark foliage and hooked brown prickles. It blooms throughout summer, taking only brief breaks between periods of flower production.

Lilian Austin blooms all summer with stunning, fragrant, salmon–pink flowers.

TIPS

* Plant this rose at the front of flowerbeds to take advantage of its low, spreading habit and flowers that spill over onto a pathway. A group of three makes an outstanding display.

* Lilian Austin is a very reliable, disease-resistant variety. It is one of the fastest-selling English roses at our greenhouse.

* This variety was introduced in 1973, and was named after the mother of breeder David Austin. He describes these flowers as semi-double, likely because they open fully to expose the stamens, but we consider them to be double, owing to the large number of petals.

Little Artist

Miniature Rose

L ittle Artist is an apt name for this miniature rose. Like its parent Eyepaint (see page 182), this variety has unusual flowers that are termed 'hand-painted.' Each flower opens creamy white with brushmark streaks of red, and then gradually transforms to solid red, except at the centre and on the undersides of petals. Bright yellow stamens complete the picture.

Official Colour •
  red blend
Form • semi-double
Scent • mild apple
  fragrance
ARS rating • 8.5
Height • 12–18 inches
  (30–45 cm)
Spread • 12–18 inches
  (30–45 cm)
Blooms • repeatedly
  from early summer
  to frost

TENDER

201

TIPS

* Little Artist blooms profusely with long-lasting, 1- to 1 1/2-inch (2.5–3.5 cm) flowers in bright, unfading colours. The first flowers of the season are the most vivid.

* This variety is noted for its superb disease resistance. It was introduced in 1982.

Watching Little Artist's flowers change colour is like seeing a blank canvas transformed into a work of art.

Floribunda Rose

TENDER

202

Official Colour •
  orange blend
Form • double
Scent • fruity
ARS rating • (—)
Height •
  2–3 feet (60–90 cm)
Spread •
  2–3 feet (60–90 cm)
Blooms • repeatedly
  from early summer
  to frost

Livin' Easy

Livin' Easy is one of the newest floribundas, and has been highly rated in garden tests across North America. This low-maintenance rosebush produces scads of large, fragrant, apricot-orange, double flowers, each 4 inches (10 cm) across, with slightly ruffled petals. Livin' Easy blooms consistently and profusely all season, with bright, showy flowers offset by glossy, bright green, disease-resistant foliage.

TIPS

* This is a 'self-cleaning' variety, which means the petals fall cleanly from finished flowers, resulting in a tidier bush, although deadheading is still required if you want more blooms.

* Expect consistently great performance and loads of flowers from this rose, which grows in gardens across North America.

* Livin' Easy was introduced in 1996 and won the AARS award the same year.

Loving Touch

Miniature Rose

I f you like pastel colours, as I do, you will love Loving Touch. Its creamy apricot flowers are large for a miniature variety, and they have the tight, spiral form of the long-stemmed roses you find at florists. Loving Touch blooms abundantly all summer, putting on a splendid show in flowerbeds or patio pots. It is one of the few miniature roses that produces rosehips.

Official Colour • apricot   TENDER
Form • double   203
Scent • light 'tea rose'
   fragrance
ARS rating • 8.6
Height • 12–18 inches
   (30–45 cm)
Spread • 12–18 inches
   (30–45 cm)
Blooms • repeatedly
   from early summer
   to frost

TIPS

* These flowers turn deeper apricot in cooler temperatures. For the best flower colour, plant the rosebush in an open site that is sunny but not hot.

* This variety was introduced in 1982 and won the ARS Award of Excellence for Miniature Roses in 1985.

Loving Touch is a choice miniature variety, with high–centred flowers of rich apricot.

Magic Carrousel

Miniature Rose

TENDER

204

Official Colour • red
  blend
Form • semi-double
Scent • light
ARS rating • 9.0
Height • 18–22 inches
  (45–55 cm)
Spread • 18–22 inches
  (45–55 cm)
Blooms • repeatedly
  from early summer
  to frost

Magic Carrousel is stunning in borders, flowerbeds or patio pots because it is absolutely covered in unique, bicoloured flowers. The white petals of these 2-inch (5 cm) flowers are outlined in rosy red, and flatten as they open, exposing the yellow stamens. Since it was introduced in 1972, Magic Carrousel has become one of the best-known miniature varieties. These lovely little flowers have a mild, sweet fragrance somewhat like that of violets.

Magic Carrousel is an eye-catching miniature rose with a profusion of striking red–and–white flowers.

TIPS

* Flowers tend to be quite pink when they first open, and fade to white as they age, resulting in different hues on the bush at the same time.

* For best flower colour, plant this disease-resistant variety in a site that is sunny but not too hot. Avoid flowerbeds near heat-radiating brick walls, or against a reflective surface, such as white stucco.

* If you can bear to cut them from the bush, these roses make good cutflowers. They are sometimes borne one to a stem, and sometimes in clusters of three.

* Magic Carrousel won the ARS Award of Excellence for Miniature Roses in 1975.

Mary Rose

Mary Rose is often the first English rose to bloom and the last to stop. This variety has large, warm rose-pink, rounded flowers in clusters of two to five. I find that these flowers, unlike most roses, tend to darken with age. Mary Rose continues to bloom into fall, sometimes with a paler colour. Its fragrance is less powerful than most English roses, but there are loads of 4- to 5-inch (10–12.5 cm) flowers. This is a graceful, bushy, exceptionally thorny shrub with excellent disease resistance.

Official Colour •
    medium pink
Form • double
Scent • light, sweet
    'damask' fragrance
ARS rating • 8.7
Height •
    4 feet (1.2 m)
Spread •
    3–4 feet (90–120 cm)
Blooms • repeatedly
    from early summer
    to frost

TIPS

❀ Deadhead regularly until a few weeks before the end of summer to keep plants tidy and to promote further blooming.

❀ Cut these flowers for bouquets. You can often find a fat rosebud alongside a fully opened flower, which creates a pretty picture in a vase.

❀ This is one of the hardier English roses, but mulching for winter is still recommended (see page 62).

❀ Mary Rose was introduced in 1983. It was named after Henry VIII's flagship, the *Mary Rose*, which sank during battle near the Isle of Wight in 1545. The ship was recovered in 1982, after having spent over 400 years at the bottom of the sea.

✳ *Mary Rose blooms longer than most English roses, with very double, very large flowers.*

Minnie Pearl

Miniature Rose

TENDER

206

Official Colour •
pink blend
Form • double
Scent • light
ARS rating • 9.4
Height • 14–20 inches
(35–50 cm)
Spread • 14–20 inches
(35–50 cm)
Blooms • repeatedly
from early summer
to frost

✺ *Minnie Pearl is the ARS's highest-rated miniature rose.*

Minnie Pearl is an attractive miniature rose, studded with shapely, 1-inch (2.5 cm), double flowers of warm coral-pink with darker edges and undersides. It was named after the world-famous country comedian, best known for her trademark greeting 'Howw-deeeeeeeee' as well as her large-brimmed straw hat with the $1.95 price tag still attached. Whether or not you were a fan, this vigorous rose will make you smile with its undemanding beauty.

TIPS

❋ Plant this heat-loving variety in a warm, sunny spot, such as in a flowerbed against the south side of your house.

❋ Snip off finished flowers to keep plants tidy and encourage further blooming.

❋ Minnie Pearl was introduced in 1982; its famed namesake passed away in 1996 at age 83.

Miss All-American Beauty

Hybrid Tea Rose

W ith very full, double flowers up to 5 inches (12.5 cm) across and a heavy perfume, Miss All-American Beauty is a knockout. One of this variety's unique features is its consistently pure, strong colour. The long-lasting flowers hold the same, unfading shade of deep rich pink from the time rosebuds form until petals drop. Miss All-American Beauty is a vigorous, attractive bush, with huge, leathery leaves.

Official Colour •
  dark pink
Form • double
Scent • strong 'tea rose'
  fragrance
ARS rating • 8.2
Height • 3–4 feet
  (90–120 cm)
Spread • 2¹/₂–3 feet
  (75–90 cm)
Blooms • repeatedly
  from early summer
  to frost

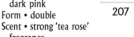

TENDER
207

TIPS

* The flower colour of many roses fades rather quickly, but this variety retains its strong colour even in hot weather.

* In poor weather, Miss All-American Beauty doesn't bloom well, but when the sun shines, these flowers are outstanding!

* Sometimes you'll find one flower per stem, and sometimes clusters. Miss All-American Beauty makes a good cutflower.

* This disease-resistant variety was introduced in 1965 and was an AARS winner in 1968. It is also known as Maria Callas.

Miss All–American Beauty has huge, very fragrant flowers, with strong, consistent colour.

Mister Lincoln

Official Colour •
dark red
Form • double
Scent • very strong
'damask' fragrance
ARS rating • 8.8
Height • 4–4 1/2 feet
(1.2–1.4 m)
Spread • 2–2 1/2 feet
(60–75 cm)
Blooms • repeatedly
from early summer
to frost

Mister Lincoln is one of the few hybrid roses that customers at our greenhouses ask for by name. But even gardeners who are unfamiliar with this award-winning variety are immediately won over at first sight of its immense, deep velvety red flowers, making it easily the most popular red rose. The fragrant flowers are huge, up to 5 1/2 inches (13 cm) across, with 8 to 10 flowers on each long stem—perfect for elegant bouquets!

TIPS

* The fragrance of just one of these flowers fills an entire room with sweet perfume. To remove the hooked thorns, push them sideways with your thumb after cutting the flowers.

* Mister Lincoln is a tough, dependable rose with excellent disease resistance. It is one of the hardier hybrid teas, although it still requires winter protection. The Mister Lincoln in our garden is now over 12 years old.

* This variety was introduced in 1964 and won the AARS award in 1965.

Although there are no black roses, Mister Lincoln has one of the darkest hues of all roses, as well as a very strong fragrance.

Nearly Wild

T he only 'wild' thing about Nearly Wild is its prolific bloom at the beginning of the season. It blooms so profusely in late spring to early summer that you can barely see the foliage for the flowers. Bright pink, single flowers are 1½ to 2 inches (3.5–5 cm) across, with a light, sweet-apple fragrance. Nearly Wild looks similar to our Alberta wild roses, but unlike them, continues to bloom non-stop until fall frost.

Official Colour •
  medium pink
Form • single
Scent • light, sweet
ARS rating • 7.6
Height •
  1½ feet (45 cm)
Spread •
  2 feet (60 cm)
Blooms • repeatedly
  from late spring
  to frost

TIPS

* Plant this rose in mixed flowerbeds, or highlight its flowers against a background of evergreen shrubs.

* This variety is susceptible to blackspot. To help prevent this disease, water at the base of the plant rather than from overhead, and avoid wetting the foliage.

* Because Nearly Wild is quite cold-hardy, I don't prune in fall. I just provide a protective mulch and then prune my rosebush in spring. Usually a fair bit of the old wood survives winter. (See *What to Do in Fall, Winter & Spring* on page 61.)

* Nearly Wild is one of the oldest floribunda varieties still available. It was introduced in 1941.

Nearly Wild is one of the hardiest floribundas, and is one of the first roses to bloom in spring.

Olympiad

Hybrid Tea Rose

Official Colour •
medium red
Form • double
Scent • light, fruity
ARS rating • 9.1
Height • 3–4 feet
(90–120 cm)
Spread • 2 ½–3 feet
(75–90 cm)
Blooms • repeatedly
from early summer
to frost

Olympiad is a superb rose that few can resist. Its large, double flowers are exceptionally long lasting, and retain their unfading, true red colour until they drop to the ground. Thick, velvety petals remain unblemished by rain, and the rosebuds are so dark that they are almost black. Olympiad is a bushy, upright shrub with thorny canes, distinctive grey-green foliage and long, strong stems that each hold just one perfect red rose.

TIPS

* For best performance, avoid planting in hot areas of the garden.

* Olympiad is an excellent cutflower, generally lasting about 10 days after cutting.

* This rosebush has excellent resistance to both blackspot and powdery mildew.

* Introduced in 1982, Olympiad was an AARS winner in 1984 and won the Portland Gold Medal in 1985. It is one of the American Rose Society's highest-rated hybrid tea roses.

Olympiad is one of the reddest roses, with 4- to 5-inch (10–12.5 cm), velvety flowers that are very long lasting both on the bush and in the vase. Flower size increases in cool weather.

Painted Moon

I fell in love with Painted Moon at first sight. Its 3- to 4-inch (7.5–10 cm), cupped, double flowers are a rich rosy-red, a shade that reminds me of watermelons. When flowers first open, the central petals are yellow-gold, gradually changing to peach, apricot and pale cream as flowers age. The effect is pleasing, unlike that of some roses, which fade to unpleasant colours. Painted Moon is a stocky, upright shrub with handsome, semi-glossy foliage.

TIPS

* Painted Moon produces lots of flowers, usually in small clusters, throughout the season. The flowers are borne one to a stem.

* Painted Moon is a good cutflower. Cut when flowerbuds are loose but not yet open. Bouquets usually last about a week.

* This variety was introduced in 1989.

🌺 *Painted Moon is a beautiful rose with a glowing blend of colours.*

Hybrid Tea Rose

Official Colour •
  red blend
Form • double
Scent • light 'tea rose'
  fragrance
ARS rating • (—)
Height • 3–3¹/₂ feet
  (90–105 cm)
Spread • 2¹/₂–3 feet
  (75–90 cm)
Blooms • repeatedly
  from early summer
  to frost

Paradise

Official Colour • mauve
Form • double
Scent • fruity
ARS rating • 8.3
Height • 3–4 feet
(90–120 cm)
Spread • 2¹/₂–3 feet
(75–90 cm)
Blooms • repeatedly
from early summer
to frost

Paradise has one of the most unusual colour combinations, with large, silvery–lavender flowers edged in ruby–red.

Paradise is a rose that cannot be ignored, and people either love or hate its bold combination of colours. These large, double flowers have perfectly arranged lavender petals splashed in ruby-red and spiralled around pinkish centres. Paradise blooms well all season, with deliciously scented flowers that are from 3¹/₂ to 4¹/₂ inches (8.5–11 cm) across.

TIPS

* Heat brings out the best flower colour, but avoid planting this variety in very hot areas of the garden. Reflected heat from a brick or white stucco wall may cause foliage to become sunburnt.

* Paradise can be susceptible to powdery mildew. To help prevent this disease, water in the morning rather than at night, and don't crowd the plants; good air circulation helps ward it off.

* Introduced in 1978, Paradise won both the AARS award and the Portland Gold Medal in 1979. It is also known as Burning Sky.

Pascali

I f you like white roses, you will love Pascali. This rose just keeps getting better. Six years after it was introduced in 1963, it won the AARS award. In 1991, almost 30 years later, this variety was named by the World Federation of Rose Societies as 'World's Favourite Rose,' one of only eight roses to ever be so honoured. Pascali's long-lasting, double flowers are 4 to 4$^1/_2$ inches (10–11 cm) across, with tightly spiralled centres and long, straight stems. Dark green, leathery foliage enhances the abundant flowers.

Official Colour • white
Form • double
Scent • light, fresh, sweet
ARS rating • 8.1
Height • 3$^1/_2$–4 feet (1–1.2 m)
Spread • 2$^1/_2$–3 feet (75–90 cm)
Blooms • repeatedly from early summer to frost

TENDER

213

TIPS

* Avoid planting in a very hot area of the garden. Pascali prefers cooler conditions, and performs best in a sunny, open site with good air circulation.

* Occasionally, this variety may get blackspot. To help prevent this fungal disease, avoid wetting the foliage. Water at the base of the plant rather than from overhead.

* These perfect white roses make exceptionally long-lasting cutflowers that seem to grow in the vase. For bouquets that last up to twice as long as most other roses, cut when the flowers are just beginning to open.

Pascali is the best white rose for purity of colour and superb cutflowers.

Hybrid Tea Rose

Paul Shirville

Official Colour •
    orange-pink
Form • double
Scent • sweet
ARS rating • 8.0
Height • 2¹/₂–3 feet
    (75–90 cm)
Spread • 2 ¹/₂ feet
    (75 cm)
Blooms • repeatedly
    from early summer
    to frost

If you want lots and lots of fragrant flowers from an undemanding rosebush, Paul Shirville is the variety for you. From early summer through fall, it blooms with rosy salmon-pink flowers, which are each 3 to 3¹/₂ inches (7.5–8.5 cm) across, borne one to a stem or in clusters of three. This vigorous, low sprawling shrub is graced with large, healthy, semi-glossy, dark green leaves and reddish prickles.

TIPS

* These fragrant flowers are spectacular in bouquets. They last about a week. For the strongest scent, cut the flowers early in the morning.

* The flower petals stand up well to wind and rain.

* Paul Shirville is one of the most cold-hardy hybrid tea roses.

* This disease-resistant variety was introduced in 1981 and won the Edland Fragrance Medal in 1982.

Paul Shirville blooms all season with masses of sweetly scented, double roses.

Peace

Hybrid Tea Rose

Gardeners or not, I find that most people know the rose Peace. It is one of the oldest hybrid teas still available, and was the first rose to be named as 'World's Favourite Rose' by the World Federation of Rose Societies in 1976. Peace blooms profusely with large, very double flowers of rich yellow, edged in rose-pink. It was launched to commemorate the end of World War II with the words: 'The greatest new rose of our time should be named for the world's greatest desire—peace.'

Official Colour •
  yellow blend
Form • double
Scent • light, fruity
ARS rating • 8.6
Height • 3 feet (90 cm)
Spread • 3 feet (90 cm)
Blooms • repeatedly
  from early summer
  to frost

TENDER

215

TIPS

❁ Peace is a good cutflower, with huge, 6-inch (15 cm) flowers that look stunning in bouquets.

❁ This variety is one of the hardiest hybrid tea roses. It still needs winter protection, but ours has continued to thrive for 14 years now without it.

❁ Peace has won numerous awards, including the Portland Gold Medal in 1944, AARS in 1946, ARS Gold Medal in 1947 and The Golden Rose of the Hague in 1965.

❁ This variety was bred by the famous Meilland rose-breeding family of France, and was originally named Mme. A. Meilland. It is also known as Gloria Dei and Gioia.

Peace is the most popular hybrid tea rose in the world. No two of these opulent roses are exactly alike in their blends of colour.

English Rose

TENDER

Official Colour •
    light pink
Form • semi-double
Scent • fragrant
ARS rating • (—)
Height •
    3–4 feet (90–120 cm)
Spread •
    3 feet (90 cm)
Blooms • repeatedly
    from early summer
    to frost

Peach Blossom

P each Blossom is stunning in full bloom. It becomes covered in masses of fragrant flowers that have satiny, blush-pink petals and bright yellow stamens. New foliage is red, changing to medium green, accentuating the small clusters of 3- to 4-inch (7.5–8.5 cm) flowers. Peach Blossom blooms in waves all summer.

TIPS

* Have patience with young plants. It may take two or three years after planting for this variety to reach its full potential.

* To prolong flowering, deadhead regularly until a few weeks before the end of summer. Peach Blossom is one of the few English roses that produces a good crop of rosehips.

* Peach Blossom was introduced in 1990. Despite its name, neither the flowers nor the fragrance really resemble the blossoms of a peach tree.

Peach Blossom blooms with a profusion of dainty, fragrant flowers.

Pink Parfait

Grandiflora Rose

Because Pink Parfait has longer petals than most grandiflora roses, its flowers look very elegant—almost aristocratic. This variety starts blooming a bit later than most others, but then puts on a splendid display from midsummer on, with abundant clusters of 3¹/₂- to 4-inch (8.5–10 cm), double flowers in pretty, soft colours. These flowers are varying shades of pink, from medium to pale, blended light orange at the centre and flushed cream at the base.

Official Colour • pink blend
Form • double
Scent • light
ARS rating • 8.2
Height • 4–4¹/₂ feet (1.2–1.4 m)
Spread • 3–3¹/₂ feet (90–105 cm)
Blooms • repeatedly from early summer to frost

TIPS

❋ Flower colour tends to fade in hot weather.

❋ Cut these flowers for charming bouquets that last about a week. I like to display them with pink baby's breath from the garden.

❋ This variety has excellent disease resistance.

❋ Pink Parfait was introduced in 1960 and won the Portland Gold Medal in 1959, the AARS award in 1961 and the Royal National Rose Society Gold Medal in 1962.

※ *Pink Parfait is a prolific bloomer, with lots of large, double flowers that make lovely bouquets.*

Hybrid Tea Rose

TENDER

Pristine

Official Colour • white
Form • double
Scent • light
ARS rating • 9.2
Height • 4–4¹/₂ feet
(1.2–1.4 m)
Spread • 3–3¹/₂ feet
(90–105 cm)
Blooms • continuously
from early summer
to frost

I love Pristine's flowers. Ivory rosebuds open to porcelain-white flowers blushed pink at the outer edges—such delicate-looking flowers are surprising from a shrub as vigorous and robust as Pristine. This tall, upright rosebush has thick, strong stems and mahogany-red new leaves that become dark green, large, waxy and tough. Each long, straight stem supports just one huge flower. Pristine is an apt name for these lovely roses.

TIPS

❀ Because this bush is so vigorous, you can cut long-stemmed roses without causing a great delay in blooming. Pristine makes a magnificent cut-flower, but drops petals quickly after opening. For the longest display, cut at the loose bud stage.

❀ Pristine is often described as nearly thornless, but the few thorns it does have are very large.

❀ This disease-resistant variety is a top-rated exhibition rose, often winning first prize at rose shows. It was introduced in 1978.

Pristine's creamy white flowers are huge, each up to 6 inches (15 cm) across.

Queen Elizabeth

Grandiflora Rose

When this variety was introduced in 1954, it was so different from any rose in existence that a new class was created, and Queen Elizabeth became the first grandiflora rose. While taller and more upright than most floribundas, Queen Elizabeth produces a similar abundance of flowers in clusters. Each flower is large, from 3½ to 4 inches (8.5–10 cm) across, with long stems like those of the hybrid teas. Queen Elizabeth remains one of the most widely grown and best loved roses, and was voted 'World's Favourite Rose' in 1979.

Official Colour • medium pink
Form • double
Scent • light 'tea rose' fragrance
ARS rating • 9.0
Height • 4–4½ feet (1.2–1.4 m)
Spread • 2½–3 feet (75–90 cm)
Blooms • repeatedly from early summer to frost

TENDER

TIPS

* Queen Elizabeth makes an excellent cutflower. Its long stems are often thornless.

* This glossy-leaved rosebush is remarkably vigorous and endures heat, humidity and insects without assistance of any kind. It has excellent resistance to blackspot and powdery mildew, but can be susceptible to rust.

* Queen Elizabeth's awards include the Portland Gold Medal in 1954, AARS in 1955, Royal National Rose Society President's International Trophy in 1955, ARS Gold Medal in 1957 and Golden Rose of the Hague in 1968.

Queen Elizabeth is one of the world's most popular roses in this century, second only to Peace.

Rainbow's End

Official Colour •
 yellow blend
Form • double
Scent • mild to none
ARS rating • 9.0
Height • 10–14 inches
 (25–35 cm)
Spread • 10–14 inches
 (25–35 cm)
Blooms • continuously
 from early summer
 to frost

Rainbow's End is a charming rose that blooms in bright, cheerful colours.

Some miniature roses are best suited to growing in pots, but Rainbow's End has a bushy, upright form, and bears its flowers on strong stems, making it one of the better miniature varieties for growing in gardens. This rosebush is never out of bloom. Pointed rosebuds open to deep yellow, $1\frac{1}{2}$-inch (3.5 cm), double flowers edged in red. The amount of red varies, and in full sun, the roses may age to entirely red. The effect is a striking, very colourful display.

TIPS

* For tips on bringing miniature roses indoors for the winter, see page 45.

* Most miniature roses take a break in blooming, but Rainbow's End continues to produce masses of flowers all summer.

* This disease-resistant variety was introduced in 1984 and won the ARS Award of Excellence for Miniature Roses in 1986.

Redouté

L ike Mary Rose, Redouté is one of the first English roses to bloom, and one of the last to stop. Redouté is a seedling or 'sport' of that variety, and identical in all respects except in its paler colour. It blooms throughout summer and into fall, with large, open, 3- to 3 1/2-inch (7.5–8.5 cm) flowers of a delicate pale pink. They make wonderful bouquets. Redouté is a bushy shrub with very thorny branches and superb disease resistance.

Official Colour •
  light pink
Form • double
Scent • light
ARS rating • (—)
Height • 3–4 feet
  (90–120 cm)
Spread • 3–3 1/2 feet
  (90–105 cm)
Blooms • continuously
  from early summer
  to frost

TENDER

TIPS

* To keep plants tidy and promote further blooming, deadhead regularly until a few weeks before the end of summer.

* Redouté is a lovely cutflower. For the longest vase life, cut when rosebuds are loosely open.

* This variety was introduced in 1992. It is named after Pierre Joseph Redouté (1759–1840), an artist famous for his watercolour paintings of roses in the Empress Joséphine's garden at Malmaison, France.

Redouté is one of the longest–blooming English roses.

Floribunda Rose

Official Colour •
pink blend
Form • semi-double
Scent • sweet apple
fragrance
ARS rating • 8.5
Height • 2–2¹/₂ feet
(60–75 cm)
Spread • 2 feet
(60 cm)
Blooms • repeatedly
from early summer
to frost

Regensberg

A t times, Regensberg blooms so profusely that the foliage is almost completely covered by clusters of fragrant flowers. These distinctive flowers are called 'hand-painted,' because they look as if someone had drawn a paintbrush across the upper surface of the bright white petals, leaving behind streaks of hot rose-pink. The 4¹/₂-inch (11 cm) flowers open to expose yellow stamens surrounded by white eyes. As flowers age, the pink softens to a gentler hue. No two flowers ever look exactly the same.

TIPS

❀ Avoid planting this rose in hot areas of the garden. Flowers will be larger in a cooler but sunny site.

❀ This low, bushy rose looks wonderful in planters or patio pots. See *Growing Roses in Patio Pots* on page 43 for details on care.

❀ Introduced in 1979, this disease-resistant variety was named after the German city of Regensberg. This rose won the Baden-Baden Gold Medal in 1980. It is also known as Buffalo Bill or Young Mistress.

❀ *Regensberg has uncommon, 'hand-painted' flowers that are unusually large for a floribunda.*

Rise 'n' Shine

Miniature Rose

S ome rose varieties like more heat than others, and Rise 'n' Shine is one of those that performs best in a warm, sunny site. Plant this bright miniature variety in a patio pot on your sunny back deck, where its abundance of rich yellow, double flowers will greet you each morning. Unlike most miniature roses, which have little to no scent, Rise 'n' Shine emits a lovely fruity scent.

Official Colour •
  medium yellow
Form • double
Scent • fruity
ARS rating • 9.1
Height • 10–14 inches
  (25–35 cm)
Spread • 10–14 inches
  (25–35 cm)
Blooms • repeatedly
  from early summer
  to frost

TIPS

* Keep plants tidy and encourage more flowers by deadheading regularly until a few weeks before the end of summer.

* With its long, pointed rosebuds, dark green leaves and nicely formed, 1 ½-inch (3.5 cm) flowers in the classic hybrid tea form, Rise 'n' Shine is a popular variety with gardeners who like to enter flower shows.

* This disease-resistant variety was introduced in 1977, and won the ARS Award of Excellence for Miniature Roses the following year.

Rise 'n' Shine is the best of the yellow miniature roses, with a profusion of flowers. It is one of the very few fragrant roses in its category.

Royal Highness

Official Colour •
  light pink
Form • double
Scent • light 'tea rose'
  fragrance
ARS rating • 8.2
Height • 3 1/2–4 feet
  (1–1.2 m)
Spread • 3 feet
  (90 cm)
Blooms • repeatedly
  from early summer
  to frost

*Royal Highness is
a superb rose for cutting,
with huge, beautiful, long–
stemmed flowers.*

When you grow Royal Highness, you know you
have a real rose. Long, pointed rosebuds open to
very full, high-centred, double flowers, which are held
regally upright on long, straight, thick stems. Each
flower is from 5 to 5 1/2 inches (12.5–13.5 cm) across, in
the palest possible shade that can still be called pink.
The frosted petals remain unblemished after rainshowers.
The dark, glossy, leathery foliage offsets these long-
lasting flowers.

TIPS

* With its long-stemmed flowers, Royal Highness
  looks lovely in bouquets.

* To help prevent powdery mildew, water in the
  morning rather than at night, and don't crowd
  the plants; good air circulation helps ward off
  this disease. Royal Highness can also be
  susceptible to rust.

* Although this variety is less winter-hardy than
  some hybrid teas, our Royal Highness rosebush
  is now over 10 years old.

* This variety was introduced in 1962. It won the
  Portland Gold Medal in 1960, Madrid
  Gold Medal in 1962, and was an
  AARS winner in 1963.

St. Patrick

L ooking for something different to add to your garden? St. Patrick is a lovely new rose with unusual flowers tinged in green. We first saw it at another nursery where it was being tested before it became available for sale, and we were most impressed with its striking colour and abundance of blooms. Apple-green rosebuds open to 3- to 3^1/$_2$-inch (7.5–8.5 cm), double flowers that are lemon-yellow in colour and flushed with gold and pale mint-green. St. Patrick's flowers open slowly and remain fresh-looking, providing a long-lasting, showy display.

Official Colour •
  yellow blend
Form • double
Scent • light
ARS rating • (—)
Height •
  3–4 feet (90–120 cm)
Spread •
  3–4 feet (90–120 cm)
Blooms • all summer
  to frost

TENDER

225

Tips

* Plant this variety in a warm, sunny area of the garden to bring out the green tones of its stunning flowers. The amount of green on flowers varies with temperature: when it's warmer, flowers are greener, and when it's cooler, the flowers take on touches of gold.

 *With its green–tinted flowers, St. Patrick is one of the most unusual roses.*

* St. Patrick has unusually thick petals, a rare quality for roses in general and for yellow roses in particular. The thick petals result in flowers that stand up well to wind, rain and heat. They last longer both in gardens and bouquets.

* This variety has excellent resistance to powdery mildew and blackspot.

* St. Patrick was introduced in 1996 and was an AARS winner the same year. The 'luck of the Irish' must have been behind this unique, green-tinted rose, for St. Patrick is only the second variety from an amateur breeder to ever win an AARS award.

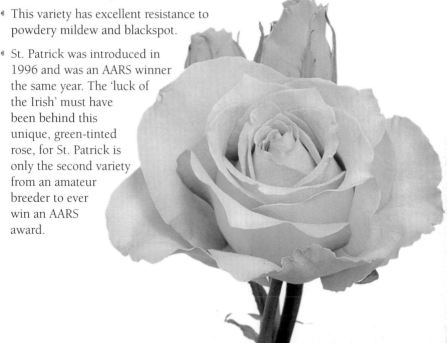

English Rose

TENDER

Official Colour •
light pink
Form • double
Scent • very strong,
spicy
ARS rating • (—)
Height • 3–3 1/2 feet
(90–105 cm)
Spread • 2 1/2–3 feet
(75–90 cm)
Blooms • repeatedly
from early summer
to frost

St. Swithun

*'St. Swithun's Day, if ye do rain
for forty days it will remain.'*

July 15 is St. Swithun's Day, a date that, for the British, is comparable to our Groundhog Day. Legend has it that St. Swithun, the patron saint of Winchester Cathedral, asked to be buried outside under 'the sweet rain of heaven.' Centuries later, when clerics tried to move his remains inside the church, the saint sent a torrential 40-day downpour. The rose named in his honour is one of the most fragrant English roses, with large, soft cherry-pink flowers throughout summer.

TIPS

* Plant this variety near a walkway, outdoor seating area or under a window that is often open, in order to best enjoy its fragrance.

* St. Swithun is a vigorous, bushy, disease-resistant shrub that holds its flowers well above the foliage.

* Cut these 3- to 3 1/2-inch (7.5–8.5 cm) flowers for bouquets. They have a delicious, spicy myrrh perfume that fills the room with fragrance.

* This variety was introduced in 1993, and is one of the newest English roses.

English roses are generally more fragrant than most roses, and St. Swithun is one of the most highly fragrant English roses.

Sally Holmes

A flowerbed full of Sally Holmes in full bloom is truly an impressive sight. Very large, heavy clusters of 3 1/2-inch (8.5 cm), single roses are held on upright stems. The creamy white petals are accented by showy yellow stamens, pale apricot-pink flowerbuds and dark glossy foliage. This variety blooms repeatedly throughout summer and well into fall. The flowers have a very delicate perfume.

Official Colour •
   creamy white
Form • single
Scent • light, sweet
ARS rating • 8.5
Height •
   3–4 feet (90–120 cm)
Spread •
   3 feet (90 cm)
Blooms • repeatedly
   from early summer
   to frost

TENDER

227

TIPS

* Although petals fall cleanly from finished flowers, resulting in a tidier bush, deadheading is still required to encourage further blooming.

* In the southern United States, Sally Holmes grows as a climber, but in our area, we grow it as a shrub.

* This variety was introduced in 1976.

With big clusters of large flowers, Sally Holmes makes an impressive display.

Hybrid Tea Rose

Official Colour •
pink blend
Form • double
Scent • very strong
spiced-fruit fragrance
ARS rating • (—)
Height • 3–3$^1/_2$ feet
(90–105 cm)
Spread • 2$^1/_2$–3 feet
(75–90 cm)
Blooms • repeatedly
from early summer
to frost

Secret

S ecret's fragrance is so powerful that the aroma from just one rosebush can fill your entire garden. The rich fragrance is an entrancing combination of spicy, fruity and sweet. This variety produces armloads of slightly frilled, double flowers in pale cream with a pink blush and dark pink edges, each up to 4$^1/_2$ inches (11 cm) across. One of the best things about Secret is that even young plants bloom well—the same year that we planted ours, the bush was absolutely covered with flowers!

TIPS

* For the largest flower size, avoid planting this variety in hot areas of the garden.

* These long-stemmed roses are wonderful in bouquets. Most often there is one flower per stem but once in a while you'll find small clusters.

* This variety was introduced in 1992 and was an AARS winner in 1994. It has high disease resistance, especially to powdery mildew.

❋ *Secret is among the most fragrant roses, with a strong, spiced–fruit perfume.*

Sexy Rexy

Floribunda Rose

Official Colour • medium pink
Form • double
Scent • light, fresh
ARS rating • 9.0
Height • 2–2½ feet (60–75 cm)
Spread • 2 feet (60 cm)
Blooms • early and late summer

Sexy Rexy is absolutely covered with massive clusters of ruffled, very full flowers like shell-pink powder-puffs. As many as 100 flowers, each 2½ to 3 inches (6–7.5 cm) across, bloom at once! These flowers are long lasting, with petals that don't discolour in rain. Sexy Rexy blooms in early summer and then takes a long break before blooming again with another outstanding show of flowers in late summer.

Tips

- Sexy Rexy is one of the smaller floribunda bushes. With its spreading branches and glossy, light green foliage, it looks attractive in a flowerbed even when not blooming.
- Because of its size, this rose is suited to growing in patio pots. See page 43 for details on growing roses in pots.
- Sexy Rexy has good disease resistance, and is often used by rose breeders who are creating new varieties, because it is known to pass on this trait.
- This variety was introduced in 1984 and won the New Zealand Gold Medal the same year. It is also known as Heckenzauber.

Sexy Rexy is a beautiful rose and a profuse bloomer.

Showbiz

Official Colour •
medium red
Form • semi-double
Scent • light to none
ARS rating • 8.6
Height •
2–3 feet (60–90 cm)
Spread •
2 feet (60 cm)
Blooms • repeatedly
from early summer
to frost

Showbiz is one of the most brilliant red floribundas.

Many gardeners tell me that they want a smaller rosebush that would fit nicely in a shrub bed. Floribundas are generally good choices, because of their compact form and abundant flowers. Showbiz is a particularly colourful variety, with long-lasting, large, fire-engine red flowers in massive clusters. All the flowers in the cluster tend to open at once, resulting in a far showier display than in many varieties on which flowers in the cluster open progressively, one or two at a time.

TIPS

* With its masses of 2 $\frac{1}{2}$- to 3-inch (6–7.5 cm) flowers, Showbiz makes a splendid display in patio pots. Profuse clusters of unfading flowers almost completely cover the glossy foliage. For details on growing pot roses, see page 43.

* Remove the entire cluster after flowering to encourage more blooms. Stop deadheading a few weeks before the end of summer to allow the bush to slow its growth down before winter.

* Be sure to cut these flowers for long-lasting bouquets.

* Showbiz was introduced in 1983 and became an AARS winner in 1985. It is currently North America's top-rated exhibition rose in the floribunda category.

* This disease-resistant rose has a curious collection of seemingly unrelated names, like Ingrid Weibull and Bernhard Daneke.

Snow Bride

Miniature Rose

Official Colour • white
Form • semi-double
Scent • light
ARS rating • 9.3
Height • 12–16 inches
  (30–40 cm)
Spread • 12–16 inches
  (30–40 cm)
Blooms • repeatedly
  from early summer
  to frost

TENDER
231

This charming miniature rose looks as if it belongs in a wedding bouquet. To create this effect in your garden, plant Snow Bride in a large container, with trailing English ivy and white lobelia around the base. One woman did up several pots in this fashion to decorate the backyard for her daughter's outdoor wedding, and to match the white roses and other flowers in the bridal bouquet.

TIPS

* Snow Bride's flowers are twice as large as the flowers from many other miniature roses, each about 2 inches (5 cm) across.

* Avoid planting in extremely hot sites, such as near heat-reflecting white stucco walls or on sun-baked decks. This variety does best in moderate temperatures.

* In 1983, the year after it was introduced, Snow Bride won the ARS Award of Excellence for Miniature Roses.

Snow Bride is an out-standing miniature rose with large, creamy white flowers.

Sonia

Grandiflora Rose

TENDER

232

Official Colour •
   pink blend
Form • double
Scent • fruity
ARS rating • 8.1
Height • 3–3 1/2 feet
   (90–105 cm)
Spread • 2–2 1/2 feet
   (60–75 cm)
Blooms • repeatedly
   from early summer
   to frost

If you see a salmon-pink, long-stemmed rose at a florist's shop, it is likely Sonia. This variety was originally created for the cutflower market, and more than 20 years later, it is still the most popular florist's rose in this colour. Most florist roses don't do well in the garden, but Sonia is an exception, because it has also become one of the most popular gardener's roses. As far as I know, this rose is the only variety to be considered one of the best in both categories.

TIPS

* Avoid planting this rose in hot sites, such as flowerbeds alongside brick walls or reflective surfaces. Heat causes the 4- to 4 1/2-inch (10–11 cm) flowers to be smaller.

* Because this rosebush doesn't grow very large in our climate, the stems will be shorter than florists' roses. It is best to cut as little of the stem as possible if you want more flowers on your bush that season—taking off too much stem prevents or delays flowering. Sonia looks just as lovely in a rosebowl or short bouquet.

* Sonia has excellent disease resistance to both powdery mildew and blackspot.

* Introduced in 1974, this variety was named after the granddaughter of the rose breeder who created the Peace rose.

Sonia is one of the best cutflowers, and is the only garden rose that is also widely sold by florists.

Starina

Despite its official colour designation of 'orange-red,' Starina's double flowers are actually a glowing blend of deep, warm hues, including carmine, orange and scarlet, with yellow at the base of each petal. This variety looks like a miniature hybrid tea rose, with its pointed rosebuds and classic flowers that are only 1 1/2 inches (3.5 cm) across. Once you see this rounded, glossy-leaved rosebush, it is easy to understand why Starina was, for many years, the most popular of all miniature roses for exhibition.

Official Colour •
   orange-red
Form • double
Scent • light
ARS rating • 9.0
Height • 12–16 inches
   (30–40 cm)
Spread • 12–16 inches
   (30–40 cm)
Blooms • repeatedly
   from early summer
   to frost

TIPS

* Starina is an easy-to-grow, reliable, disease-resistant miniature rose that consistently produces lots of flowers all summer. Snip off the finished flowers to keep plants tidy.

* Cut these flowers to make charming bouquets. Starina is an excellent cutflower.

* This variety was introduced in 1965, by Meilland, the same breeders who introduced the famous Peace rose. It won the Japanese Gold Medal in 1968 and the ADR award in 1971.

The unusual colour of Starina's flowers is perfectly offset by the dark, glossy foliage.

Sunsprite

Floribunda Rose

TENDER

Official Colour •
  dark yellow
Form • double
Scent • strong, sweet
  licorice fragrance
ARS rating • 8.7
Height • 2–2¹/₂ feet
  (60–75 cm)
Spread • 2–2¹/₂ feet
  (60–75 cm)
Blooms • repeatedly
  from early summer
  to frost

Sunsprite is not only one of the most fragrant roses, with an exceptionally strong scent, but also the brightest yellow.

Sunsprite is one of only nine roses in over 30 years to have been honoured with the James Alexander Gamble Award for fragrance. Only the most fragrant, outstanding new varieties are selected, after a five-year testing period. Sunsprite has a sweet licorice perfume that is powerful even at a distance, as is its brilliant, unfading colour. On a sunny day, the rich, bright yellow of these 3-inch (7.5 cm) roses is almost blinding. Individual flowers are disappointingly short lived, but Sunsprite continues to bloom with lots of double flowers all summer.

TIPS

* Though fragrant and beautiful, this is not a good rose for cutting, as petals drop quickly in the vase.

* Sunsprite is one of the most disease-free floribundas, with high resistance to both blackspot and powdery mildew.

* This rose was introduced in 1977, won the Baden-Baden Gold Medal in 1972 and the James Alexander Gamble Rose Fragrance Award in 1979.

The Alexandra Rose

English Rose

The Alexandra Rose is very different from all other English roses, which typically have very full, plump flowers. This variety stands apart with its small, starry, single flowers. These exquisite flowers are 1 1/2 to 2 inches (3.5–5 cm) across, and coppery-pink with pale yellow centres, fading gracefully to softer hues. The Alexandra Rose blooms profusely throughout summer.

Official Colour • pink blend
Form • single
Scent • light
ARS rating • (—)
Height • 4–4 1/2 feet (1.2–1.4 cm)
Spread • 3–3 1/2 feet (90–105 cm)
Blooms • continuously from early summer to frost

TIPS

❀ The Alexandra Rose grows well in partial shade.

❀ Because this rose blooms on second-year wood, prune it as little as possible. Mulch as high as possible in fall (see *Additional Care Required for Tender Roses* on page 62), and remove dead branch tips in spring.

❀ This disease-resistant variety was introduced in 1992. It is named for the British institution called the Alexandra Rose Day Charity, which in turn was named for Queen Alexandra, wife of Edward VII.

✼ *The Alexandra Rose blooms all summer, with starry flowers and refreshing colour.*

The Countryman

Official Colour •
   medium pink
Form • double
Scent • strong 'old rose'
   fragrance
ARS rating • 7.5
Height • 3–3¹/₂ feet
   (90–105 cm)
Spread • 3 feet
   (90 cm)
Blooms • repeatedly
   from early summer
   to frost

The Countryman has large flowers and a rich, heavy fragrance.

The Countryman is a lovely rose, with very fragrant, delicate-looking, rose-pink flowers on arching branches. This variety is a small rosebush that grows upright at first and then spreads its long branches outward. The flowers are 2¹/₂ to 3 inches (6–7.5 cm) across, borne in clusters of three to five. They appear to glow against the long, dark green leaves, and have a superb, rich fragrance.

TIPS

* Expect most flowers to bloom in early and late summer, with fewer flowers in between. Be sure to deadhead and fertilize, in order to encourage new growth and more blooms.

* This rose looks lovely growing in a tall pot, with its arching branches trailing over the sides. See page 43 for details on growing roses in patio pots.

* Float a flower or two in a rosebowl, in order to enjoy their sumptuous fragrance indoors.

* This variety was introduced in 1979.

The Pilgrim

The Pilgrim is a beautiful rose. Its soft, silky, very full rosettes are pale buttercream yellow, with creamy white outer petals. The rosebuds are sometimes tipped in deep crimson, resulting in the barest hints of dark colour on the pale flowers. The Pilgrim is a very upright, disease-resistant bush, with attractive, glossy foliage. It produces lots of fragrant flowers throughout summer that look as lovely in a vase as in the garden.

Official Colour •
   medium yellow
Form • double
Scent • very fragrant
ARS rating • (—)
Height • 3–3 1/2 feet
   (90–105 cm)
Spread • 3 feet
   (90 cm)
Blooms • continuously
   from early summer
   to frost

TIPS

* The Pilgrim's flowers are a softer colour than most yellow roses, so they complement almost all garden settings.

* Deadhead regularly to encourage further blooming, and cut flowers often for bouquets. The 3- to 3 1/2-inch (7.5–8.5 cm) flowers are both long lasting and fragrant in a vase.

* Introduced in 1991, The Pilgrim is one of the newer English roses. Rose breeder David Austin says it was one of the most difficult varieties to create, requiring many years of work. Because very little pollen is produced by one of the parent plants, hundreds of flowers were needed to collect enough pollen.

✻ *The Pilgrim has lovely, fragrant flowers in the softest shade of yellow.*

Hybrid Tea Rose

Tiffany

TENDER

238

Official Colour •
pink blend
Form • double
Scent • very strong,
fruity
ARS rating • 8.3
Height • 4–4¹/2 feet
(1.2–1.4 m)
Spread • 3–3¹/2 feet
(90–105 cm)
Blooms • repeatedly
from early summer
to frost

Tiffany has exceptionally long–lasting, very fragrant, large flowers.

With its profusion of large, fragrant flowers on long, sturdy stems, Tiffany has been popular for well over a quarter of a century. The long, pointed, deep pink rosebuds are touched in gold at the base, and open to perfect flowers from 4 to 5 inches (10–12.5 cm) across. The silvery pink petals have subtle touches of salmon and pale golden yellow. Flower colour changes with age and the weather. This variety is a vigorous, upright shrub with very dark, glossy foliage and somewhat thorny canes.

TIPS

* This disease-resistant rose likes heat. Plant it in a warm, sunny area of the garden for best performance and flower colour.

* With its long sturdy stems, Tiffany is a good cutflower. Usually there is just one flower per stem, but occasionally you'll find clusters. To remove thorns from stems, push them sideways with your thumb.

* Petals are silky and may become marked by rain.

* Introduced in 1954, Tiffany won the Portland Gold Medal the same year and was an AARS winner in 1955. In 1962, it became one of only nine roses to ever win the James Alexander Gamble Award for outstanding fragrance.

Touch of Class

E veryone who wanders through our garden stops
when they come to Touch of Class, to marvel at its
beauty. Salmon-pink rosebuds open to consistently
perfect flowers in warm pink with shades of coral and
cream, and bright coral on the undersides of the petals.
These double flowers are 4 to 5 inches (10–12.5 cm)
across, held proudly upright on long, sturdy stems.
New foliage and stems are reddish-green throughout
the season.

Official Colour •
  orange-pink
Scent • light 'tea rose'
  fragrance
ARS rating • 9.5
Height •
  3–4 feet (90–120 cm)
Spread •
  2–3 feet (60–90 cm)
Blooms • repeatedly
  from early summer
  to frost

TIPS

* This is an exceptionally long-lasting cutflower.
  To add variety to bouquets, cut some flowers that
  have just opened and also some still in the bud
  stage. These rosebuds last a week or longer in the
  vase, but will not continue to open.

* To help prevent blackspot, which can affect this
  variety, avoid wetting foliage. Water at the base of
  the plant rather than from overhead.

* Touch of Class was introduced in 1984, won the
  AARS award in 1986, and the Portland Gold Medal
  in 1988. This variety is currently the top-rated
  exhibition rose in North America, outranking the
  number two rose by a
  two to one margin.

Touch of Class has long-stemmed flowers that last long both on the bush and in the vase.

Trumpeter

Official Colour •
orange-red
Form • double
Scent • light, fruity
ARS rating • 8.3
Height • 2–2¹/₂ feet
(60–75 cm)
Spread • 2 feet
(60 cm)
Blooms • repeatedly
from midsummer
to frost

Trumpeter provides a stunning display with its large, brilliant orange-scarlet flowers that look like hybrid tea roses. Sometimes you'll find just one 3- to 3¹/₂-inch (7.5–8.5 cm) flower per stem, but most often these wavy-petalled flowers appear in large clusters that are heavy enough to cause branches to bow down—a charming effect! Trumpeter blooms midsummer to frost, beginning and ending its show of long-lasting flowers with a bang.

Trumpeter announces its presence with great big clusters of electric orange–red flowers.

Tips

* Plant Trumpeter in a warm, sunny location. This variety prefers a little heat. Its size and impressive flowers make it well-suited for growing in a patio pot. (See page 43 for details on caring for pot roses.)

* This is one of the shortest floribundas, with excellent resistance to both powdery mildew and blackspot.

* To encourage blooming deadhead regularly, by removing the entire cluster after flowering. Stop deadheading a few weeks before the end of summer to allow the bush to slow down its growth before winter.

* Introduced in 1977, Trumpeter won the New Zealand Gold Medal in 1977, the Portland Gold Medal in 1981 and the Royal National Rose Society Gold Medal in 1991.

Winsome

W insome blooms in a shade of purple rarely found in roses. These 1-inch (2.5 cm), double flowers are very full, and produced in abundance all season, singly or in long-stemmed clusters. The entire plant is lovely, with a bushy, rounded shape, semi-glossy, dark green foliage and big pointed rosebuds. Winsome makes a nice addition to flowerbeds, rose gardens and patio planters.

TIPS

* Winsome makes a lovely display in patio pots. I tuck a little ivy and some lobelia in a matching shade around the pot's base. For details on caring for roses in pots, refer to page 43.

* Cut these flowers for miniature bouquets.

* This variety was introduced in 1984, and won the ARS Award of Excellence for Miniature Roses in 1985. It has excellent disease resistance.

✼ *Winsome's big, deep magenta–purple flowers add unusual colour to gardens.*

Miniature Rose

Official Colour • mauve
Form • double
Scent • none
ARS rating • 8.5
Height • 16–22 inches (40–55 cm)
Spread • 16–22 inches (40–55 cm)
Blooms • repeatedly from early summer to frost

RED

'O my Luve is like a red, red rose …'
—Robert Burns (1759–96), Scottish poet

Hardy Red Roses
Adelaide Hoodless
Alexander Mackenzie
Champlain
Cuthbert Grant
F.J. Grootendorst
George Vancouver
Henry Kelsey
John Franklin
Morden Amorette
Morden Cardinette
Morden Fireglow
Morden Ruby
Quadra
The Hunter
Winnipeg Parks

Tender Red Roses
Europeana
Fisherman's Friend
L.D. Braithwaite
Mister Lincoln
Olympiad
Showbiz
Trumpeter

Europeana

PINK

Hardy Pink Roses

Autumn Damask
Cabbage Rose
Captain Samuel Holland
Celestial
Charles Albanel
Dart's Dash
David Thompson
Fimbriata
Frau Dagmar Hartopp
Frontenac
Hansa
Jens Munk
John Cabot
John Davis
Louis Jolliet

Martin Frobisher
Max Graf
Morden Blush
Morden Centennial
Nigel Hawthorne
Nozomi
Pavement Roses
Red Frau Dagmar Hartopp
Red Rugosa
Red-leaf Rose
Scabrosa
Simon Fraser
Sweetbriar Rose
Thérèse Bugnet
William Baffin

Jens Munk

If someone tells you something sub rosa, you must never reveal the secret. This expression indicates affairs in greatest confidence, and literally means 'under the rose.' It dates back to ancient Roman times, when politicians used to hang a rose from the ceiling during meetings as an emblem of their pledge of secrecy.

Tender Pink Roses

Aquarius
Charles Rennie Mackintosh
Cupcake
Dainty Bess
Electron
Elizabeth Taylor
First Prize
Gene Boerner
Gertrude Jekyll
Heritage
Mary Rose
Miss All-American Beauty
Nearly Wild
Paul Shirville
Peach Blossom
Pink Parfait
Queen Elizabeth
Redouté
Royal Highness
St. Swithun
Secret
Sexy Rexy
Sonia
The Alexandra Rose

The Countryman
Tiffany
Touch of Class

Secret

WHITE

Hardy White Roses

Alba Maxima
Alba Semi-plena
Blanc Double de Coubert
Botzaris
Double White Burnet
Frühlingsanfang
Hebe's Lip
Henry Hudson
Kakwa
Mme. Hardy
Marie Bugnet
Schneezwerg
Stanwell Perpetual
The Polar Star
White Rugosa
Wingthorn Rose

Henry Hudson

Tender White Roses

Fair Bianca
Garden Party
Glamis Castle
Gruss an Aachen
Iceberg

Pascali
Pristine
Sally Holmes
Snow Bride

Gold Medal

YELLOW

'There's a yellow rose in Texas,
I'm going there to see ...'
—AMERICAN FOLKSONG, 19TH CENTURY

Hardy Yellow Roses
Agnes
Frühlingsgold
J.P. Connell
Topaz Jewel

Tender Yellow Roses
Elina
Gold Medal
Graham Thomas
Rise 'n' Shine
St. Patrick
Sunsprite
The Pilgrim

APRICOT

Hardy Apricot Roses
Alchymist

Tender Apricot Roses
Abraham Darby
Apricot Nectar
Charles Austin
English Garden
Evelyn
Loving Touch

Loving Touch

CORAL/ORANGE

Tender Coral Orange Roses
First Edition
Folklore
Fragrant Cloud
Livin' Easy
Starina

Livin' Easy

PURPLE

Hardy Purple Roses
Alain Blanchard
Charles de Mills
Reine des Violettes
Superb Tuscan

Tender Purple Roses
Winsome

Reine des Violettes

BLENDS OF COLOUR

Eyepaint

Hardy Blended Roses

Euphrates (apricot and pink)
Frühlingsmorgen (pink and yellow)
Rosa Mundi (pink with stripes)

Tender Blended Roses

Double Delight (red and white)
Escapade (white and pink)
Eyepaint (red and white)
Granada (red and yellow)
Lilian Austin (yellow, orange and pink)
Little Artist (red and white)
Magic Carrousel (pink and white)
Minnie Pearl (pink and red)
Painted Moon (red, pink and yellow)
Paradise (pink and purple)
Peace (pink and yellow)
Rainbow's End (red and yellow)
Regensberg (pink and white)

Double Delight

An old German custom held that if a girl took one red, one pink and one white rose and steeped them in wine, she could give the potion to the object of her affection to keep him true forever.

'And the rose herself has got
Perfume which on earth is not ...'
—JOHN KEATS (1795–1821), ENGLISH POET

Rose scent is carried largely in the petals; the more petals, the stronger the scent. Double roses generally have more fragrance than single roses, but because fragrance is a recessive trait, quite a few varieties have only a very light scent or none at all. Make the most of fragrant roses by planting them along a walkway, near the back deck, close to a doorway or under a window that is often open.

Fragrant Cloud

Abraham Darby
Blanc Double de Coubert
Cabbage Rose
Double Delight
Evelyn
Fair Bianca
Fisherman's Friend
Fragrant Cloud
Gertrude Jekyll

Glamis Castle
Granada
Hansa
L.D. Braithwaite
Mme. Hardy
St. Swithun
Stanwell Perpetual
Tiffany

Fair Bianca

✳ *Rose fragrance is complex. The variety Evelyn, for example, which was produced for the British perfume company Crabtree & Evelyn, has 84 different aromatic compounds that make up its scent.*

blended colour—two or more colours on the same flower; see page 248 for a list of roses with blended colours.

bud union—the place on the lower stem where a leaf-bud of one rose has been joined to the rootstock of another rose; looks like a swollen lump, and may also be referred to as a 'graft.'

cane—a slender, woody but usually flexible stem; the word often used to describe a rose's branches.

continual bloom—flowers recurring regularly and frequently.

continuous bloom—uninterrupted or non-stop flowering.

cultivar—an abbreviation for 'cultivated variety'; a group of individual plants within a species that differ from the rest of the species.

everblooming—another term for continuous bloom.

exhibition rose—any rose flower that, when one-half to three-quarters open, exhibits the classic hybrid tea rose form: symmetrical, high centred petals arranged in an attractive, circular outline; term describing roses suitable for entering in shows or exhibitions.

hybrid—the offspring of parents of different species or varieties, with some characteristics of both parents. Most roses (except the species roses) are hybrids.

hybrid perpetual—a class of roses that was very poplar in the 1800s; derived from a class of autumn-blooming shrub roses called 'perpetuals' that are crossed with bourbon roses to produce earlier-blooming plants; Reine des Violettes is a hybrid perpetual variety.

recurrent bloom—another term for continual bloom.

repeat bloom—another term for continual bloom.

sport—a plant showing some marked variation from the normal type, usually as a result of mutation. Red Frau Dagmar Hartopp is a sport of Frau Dagmar Hartopp, and Redouté is a sport of Mary Rose. The sports have different-coloured flowers.

stamen—the pollen-bearing reproductive organs in a flower. Ninety percent of roses have yellow stamens; varieties like Dainty Bess and Frühlingsmorgen are unusual in that their stamens are burgundy.

For more information ...

If you are interested in more information about roses, contact one of the following organizations:

American Rose Society
P.O. Box 30000
Shreveport, LA 71130

Canadian Rose Society
Mrs. Anne Graber, Secretary
10 Fairfax Crescent
Scarborough, ON M1L 1Z8

Heritage Rose Society (for shrub roses)
Mr. Charles A. Walker
1512 Gorman Street
Raleigh, NC 27606

Books

Austin, David. *Old Roses and English Roses*. Woodbridge, Suffolk: The Antique Collector's Club, 1992.

Austin, David. *David Austin's English Roses*. London, England: Conran Octopus, 1993.

Beales, Peter. *Roses*. New York, NY: Henry Holt & Company, 1992.

Cairns, Thomas, ed. *Modern Roses*. Shreveport, LA: The American Rose Society, 1993.

Coggiatti, Stelvio. *Simon & Schuster's Guide to Roses*. New York, NY: Simon & Schuster, 1986.

Harkness, Jack. *Roses*. London, England: J.M. Dent & Sons, 1978.

Osborne, Robert. *Roses for Canadian Gardens*. Toronto, ON: Key Porter Books, 1991.

Phillips, Roger, and Martyn Rix, *The Random House Guide to Roses*. New York, NY: Random House, 1988.

Reddell, Rayford. *Growing Good Roses*. New York, NY: Harper & Row, 1988.

Searles, James D. *The Garden of Joy*. Great Falls, MT: Medicine River Publishing, 1990.

Taylor, Norman. *Taylor's Guide to Roses*. New York, NY: Chanticleer Press, 1986.

Magazines & Other Publications

The 1996 Handbook for Selecting Roses. American Rose Society.

Winter-hardy roses from Agriculture Canada. Agriculture Canada publication 1891/E, 1993.

Chaplin, Lois Trigg. 'Grow the Right Rose for Your Region.' *Organic Gardening*, April 1994. 56–64.

Christopher, Thomas. 'The Rugged Roses.' *National Gardening*, May/June 1994.

Ogilvie, Dr. Ian S. 'New Roses in the "Explorer" Series Released by Agriculture Canada.' In *The Canadian Rose Annual 1991*, Ethel Freeman, ed. Scarborough, On: The Canadian Rose Society, 1991.

Reddell, Rayford. 'English Roses-Jolly Good?' *American Horticulturist*, June 1993. 26–31.

Reisling, Sandra A. 'Become a Rose Breeder.' *Organic Gardening*, May/June 1993.

AARS. *See* All-American
  Rose Selections
Abraham Darby, 167
Adelaide Hoodless, 85
Agnes, 86
Alain Blanchard, 87
Alba Maxima, 88
Alba roses, 81
Alba Semi-plena, 89
Alba Suaveolens, 89
Alchymist, 90
Alexander Mackenzie, 91
All-American Rose Selections, 76
American Rose Society, 75, 76
Antique roses.
  See Old garden roses
Aphids, 54, 57, 58
Apricot Nectar, 168
Apothecary's Rose, 81, 144
Aquarius, 169
Arnaud Delbard. *See* First Edition
ARS. *See* American Rose Society
ARS rating, 76
Attar-of-roses, 72
Autumn Damask, 92
Awards for roses, 76–77

Bagged roses. *See* Boxed roses
Bare-root roses, 30, 33, 35, 50
Bernhard Daneke. *See* Showbiz
Bizarre Triumphant.
  See Charles de Mills
Blackspot, 26, 54, 55, 61, 84
Blanc Double de Coubert, 93
Blood Thorn Rose.
  See Wingthorn Rose
Blooming periods, 19–20
Botzaris, 94
Bouquets, 53, 65–67
Boxed roses, 30, 33, 35, 50
Budding, 13
Buffalo Bill. *See* Regensberg
Burning Sky. *See* Paradise
Buying roses, 29–31

Cabbage Rose, 95
Canadian Rose Society, 15
Captain Samuel Holland, 96
'Carnation' roses, 106, 107
Céleste. *See* Celestial
Celestial, 97
Champlain, 98
Charles Albanel, 99
Charles Austin, 170
Charles de Mills, 100
Charles Rennie Mackintosh, 171
Climbing roses, 37–38
Colours of flowers, 21, 66, 75,
  243–48
Container-grown roses, 30–31, 33
Cooking with roses, 70–71
  recipes, 84, 166
Crown gall, 56
Cupcake, 172
Cutflowers. *See* Bouquets
Cuthbert Grant, 101
Cuttings, 14

Dainty Bess, 173
Damask roses, 81
Dart's Dash, 102
David Thompson, 103
Deadheading, 23, 53, 54
Dianthiflora. *See* Fimbriata
Disease problems, 55–57
Donatella. *See* Granada
Double Delight, 174
Double Scots White.
  See Double White Burnet
Double Tuscany.
  See Superb Tuscan
Double Velvet. *See* Superb Tuscan
Double White Burnet, 104
Drying roses, 68
Duftwolke. *See* Fragrant Cloud
Dwarf Pavement, 137

Eglantine. *See* Sweetbriar Rose
Electron, 175
Elina, 176
Elizabeth Taylor, 177

English Garden, 178
English roses, 161–62
Escapade, 179
Euphrates, 105
Europeana, 180
Evelyn, 181
Eyepaint, 182
Explorer series roses, 79–80, 82

F.J. Grootendorst, 106
Fair Bianca, 183
Fee des Neiges. *See* Iceberg
Fertilizing, 34, 35, 49–50
  potted roses, 43
  tree roses, 41
Fimbriata, 107
First Edition, 184
First Prize, 185
Fisherman's Friend, 186
Floribunda roses, 82, 162
Foliage, colourful, 22–23
Folklore, 187
Forms of flowers, 75
Four Seasons Rose.
  See Autumn Damask
Foxi Pavement, 137
Fragrances of flowers, 20–21, 249
Fragrant Cloud, 188
Frau Dagmar Hartopp, 108
Frau Dagmar Hastrup.
  See Frau Dagmar Hartopp
French roses. *See* Gallica roses
Frontenac, 109
Fru Dagmar Hartopp.
  See Frau Dagmar Hartopp
Fru Dagmar Hastrup.
  See Frau Dagmar Hartopp
Frühlingsanfang, 110
Frühlingsgold, 111
Frühlingsmorgen, 112

Gallica roses, 81
Garden Party, 189
Gene Boerner, 190
George Vancouver, 113
Gertrude Jekyll, 191
Gioia. *See* Peace
Glamis Castle, 192
Gloria Dei. *See* Peace
Gold Medal, 193
Grafted roses, special care of, 35
Grafting, 13
Graham Thomas, 194

Granada, 195
Grandiflora roses, 163
Great White Double.
  See Alba Maxima
Grootendorst Red.
  See F.J. Grootendorst
Grootendorst Supreme, 106
Groundcover roses, 41
Gruss an Aachen, 196

Hansa, 114
Hardy roses, 79–84
  definition, 16, 79
  pruning, 53
  varieties, 85–158
Hardy shrub roses, 80
Hebe's Lip, 115
Heckenzauber. *See* Sexy Rexy
Henry Hudson, 116
Henry Kelsey, 117
Heritage, 197
History of roses, 12–13
Hulthemia persica, 135
Hybrid tea roses, 13, 82, 164

Iceberg, 198
Ingrid Weibull. *See* Showbiz
Insect problems, 57–59

J.P. Connell, 118
James Alexander Gamble
  Rose Fragrance Award, 77
Jens Munk, 119
John Cabot, 120
John Davis, 121
John Franklin, 122

Kakwa, 123

L.D. Braithwaite, 199
La France,
Lady Banks rose, 26
Leafcutter bees, 58
Lilian Austin, 200
Lipstick Rose. *See* Double Delight
Little Artist, 201
Livin' Easy, 202
Louis Jolliet, 124
Loving Touch, 203

Mme. Hardy, 125
Magic Carrousel, 204

Maria Callas.
See Miss All-American Beauty
Marie Bugnet, 126
Martin Frobisher, 127
Mary Rose, 205
Max Graf, 128
Maxima. See Alba Maxima
Mildew. See Powdery mildew
Miniature roses, 45, 165
Minnie Pearl, 206
Miss All-American Beauty, 207
Mister Lincoln, 208
Morden Amorette, 129
Morden Blush, 130
Morden Cardinette, 131
Morden Centennial, 132
Morden Fireglow, 133
Morden Ruby, 134
Mulching, 16, 33, 41, 51,
  62–63, 81

Nearly Wild, 209
Nigel Hawthorne, 135
Nozomi, 136
Nuage Perfume.
  See Fragrant Cloud

Old garden roses, 81
Old roses. See Old garden roses
Old-fashioned roses.
  See Old garden roses
Olympiad, 210

Painted Moon, 211
Paradise, 212
Parkland series roses, 82
Pascali, 213
Paul Shirville, 214
Pavement Roses, 137–38
Peace, 215
Peach Blossom, 216
Pear slugs, 59
Peat moss, 25, 34, 62
Peaudouce. See Elina
Pest control, 54–59
Phoebe's Frilled Pink.
  See Fimbriata
Pierrette Pavement, 137
Pink Grootendorst, 106
Pink Parfait, 217
Planning a rose garden, 19–23
Planting roses, 33–35
  in hedges, 38–39

Polar Star, 152
Polestar. See The Polar Star
Polstjärnan. See The Polar Star
Portland Gold Medal, 77
Potpourris, 69
Potted roses, 43–45.
  See also Tree roses
Powdery mildew, 26, 54, 55,
  56, 61
Prickly rose. See Wild rose
Pristine, 218
Pruning, 37, 51–53, 62–63
Purple Pavement, 137

Quadra, 139
Quatre Saisons.
  See Autumn Damask
Queen Elizabeth, 219
Queen of the Violets.
  See Reine des Violettes

Rainbow's End, 220
Red Frau Dagmar Hartopp, 140
Red Rugosa, 141
Red Thorn Rose.
  See Wingthorn Rose
Red-leaf Rose, 142
Redouté, 221
Regensberg, 222
Reine Blanche. See Hebe's Lip
Reine des Violettes, 143
Rise 'n' Shine, 223
Rosa
  acicularis. See Wild roses
  alba. See Alba roses
  arkansana, 82
  banksiae. See Lady Banks rose
  bracteata, 83
  x centifolia. See Cabbage Rose
  damascena. See Damask roses
  eglanteria. See Sweetbriar Rose
  fedtschenkoana, 83
  foetida, 55
  gallica. See Gallica roses
  officinalis. See Apothecary's Rose
  veriscolor. See Rosa Mundi
  glauca. See Red-leaf Rose
  kordesii, 79, 128
  rubrifolia. See Red-leaf Rose
  rugosa. See Rugosa roses
    'Alba.' See White Rugosa
  rubra. See Red Rugosa
  sericea pteracantha.
    See Wingthorn Rose
Rosa Mundi, 144

Rose curculios. *See* Rose weevils
Rose des Quatre Saisons.
  See Autumn Damask
Rose gall, 57
Rose hedges, 38–39
Rose mosaic virus, 56–57
Rose of Castille.
  See Autumn Damask
Rose weevils, 58
Rosehips, 13, 22, 23, 69, 71
Royal Highness, 224
Rubrotincta. *See* Hebe's Lip
Rugosa roses, 71, 83, 84
Rust, 55–56

St. Patrick, 225
St. Swithun, 226
Sally Holmes, 227
Sawfly larvae. *See* Pear slugs
Scabrosa, 145
Scarlet Pavement, 137
Schneewittchen. *See* Iceberg
Schneezwerg, 146
Scotch Double White.
  See Double White Burnet
Secret, 228
Semi-plena. *See* Alba Semi-plena
Sexy Rexy, 229
Shade-tolerant roses, 27
Showbiz, 230
Showy Pavement, 137
Simon Fraser, 147
Snowdwarf. *See* Schneezwerg
Snow Bride, 231
Snow Pavement, 137
Soil, 25, 49
  for potted roses, 43
Sonia, 232
Species roses, 82–83
Spider mites, 54, 57, 59
Spring Gold. *See* Frühlingsgold
Stanwell Perpetual, 148
Starina, 233
Sunsprite, 234
Superb Tuscan, 149
Superb Tuscany.
  See Superb Tuscan
Sweetbriar Rose, 150

Tender roses, 161–66
  definition, 16
  pruning, 53
  special care, 35, 62–63
  varieties, 167–241
The Alexandra Rose, 235
The Artistic Rose. *See* Dainty Bess
The Countryman, 236
The Hunter, 151
The Jacobite Rose.
  See Alba Maxima
The Pilgrim, 237
The Polar Star, 152
The Wasa Star. *See* The Polar Star
Thérèse Bugnet, 153
Thrips, 58
Tiffany, 238
Topaz Jewel, 154
Touch of Class, 239
Tree roses, 40–41
Trumpeter, 240
Tuscany Superb. *See* Superb Tuscan
Tuscany Supreme. *See* Superb Tuscan

Wasastiernan. *See* The Polar Star
Watering, 34, 47–48
  in fall, 61
  potted roses, 43
  tree roses, 40
White Rose of Finland.
  See The Polar Star
White roses.
  See Alba roses; Flower colour
White Rugosa, 155
White Star of Finland.
  See The Polar Star
Wild rose, 17
  See also Species roses
William Baffin, 156
Wingthorn Rose, 157
Winnipeg Parks, 158
Winsome, 241
Winter protection, 62
  potted roses, 44–45
  tree roses, 41
World's Favourite Rose, 77

Young Mistress. *See* Regensberg

ABOUT THE AUTHOR

Lois always finds time to speak with her customers. Here, she talks with two people in the indoor plant greenhouse.

Lois Hole and her husband Ted started selling vegetables out of their red barn more than 30 years ago; today, Hole's Greenhouses & Gardens Ltd. is one of the largest greenhouse and garden centres in Alberta. It remains a family business, owned and operated by Lois, Ted, their sons Bill and Jim, and Bill's wife Valerie.

Lois was born and raised in rural Saskatchewan, and later moved to Edmonton, Alberta. She attained a degree in Music from the Toronto Conservatory of Music.

Over the years, Lois has shared her expertise throughout Canada, writing gardening columns and speaking on radio shows and at various gardening functions. Her practical wisdom and sound advice were so much in demand that she decided to begin a series of gardening guides. The first four books in the series, *Vegetable Favorites*, *Bedding Plant Favorites*, *Perennial Favorites* and *Tomato Favorites*, have all been bestsellers. The Professional Plant Growers Association has recognized the series as an exceptional source of information by awarding it their Educational Media Award for 1995.